GENERAL CHEMISTRY STUDY GUIDE

JASMINE BRYANT, PHD

Table of Contents

UNIT 1 1

MEASUREMENT, SIGNIFICANT FIGURES, AND SCIENTIFIC NOTATION 1
PART 1: SIGNIFICANT FIGURES 1
PART 2: SCIENTIFIC NOTATION 4
PART 3: MEASUREMENT AND UNITS 5
PART 4: CONVERSION FACTORS AND DIMENSIONAL ANALYSIS 7
PRACTICE PROBLEMS 8

UNIT 2 9

QUANTUM MECHANICS AND THE ATOM 9
PART 1: ELECTROMAGNETIC RADIATION AND THE BOHR MODEL OF THE ATOM 9
PART 2: THE QUANTUM-MECHANICAL VIEW OF THE ATOM 15
PART 3: THE PERIODIC TABLE AND PERIODIC TRENDS 21
CONCEPT MAPPING 24

UNIT 3 27

CHEMICAL BONDING 27
PART 1: BONDING AND LEWIS DOT STRUCTURES 27
PART 2: MOLECULES 36
PART 3: VALENCE BOND THEORY AND HYBRIDIZATION 42
PART 4: MOLECULAR COMPOSITION 44
CONCEPT MAP 49

UNIT 4 50

STOICHIOMETRY AND REACTIONS 50
PART 1: STOICHIOMETRY OF CHEMICAL REACTIONS 50
PART 2: SOLUTIONS AND CONCENTRATION 55
PART 3: TYPES OF REACTIONS 58
CONCEPT MAP 66

UNIT 5 67

GASES 67
PART 1: THE BEHAVIOR OF GASES 67
PART 2: KINETIC MOLECULAR THEORY 74
CONCEPT MAP 78

UNIT 6 79

THERMOCHEMISTRY 79
PART 1: ENERGY, HEAT, AND WORK 79
PART 2: ENTHALPY 86
CONCEPT MAP 93

UNIT 7 94

LIQUIDS AND SOLUTIONS 94
PART 1: INTERMOLECULAR FORCES 94
PART 2: PHASE CHANGES 99
PART 3: SOLUTIONS AND SOLUBILITY 104
PART 4: COLLIGATIVE PROPERTIES 109
CONCEPT MAP 116

UNIT 8 117

MOLECULAR ORBITAL THEORY 117
PART 1: INTRODUCTION TO MOLECULAR ORBITALS 117
PART 2: MOLECULAR ORBITAL THEORY WITH P ORBITALS 122
PART 3: HETERONUCLEAR MOLECULAR ORBITALS 125

Unit 1

Measurement, Significant Figures, and Scientific Notation

Part 1: Significant Figures

Whenever we make measurements we rely on the accuracy of the tool we are using to make the measurement. Significant figure rules helps us keep track of the accuracy of our measurement as we add, subtract, multiple, and divide them to solve problems. For example, let's say we have two balances we use to weigh out samples. One balance is accurate to four decimal places and the other is only accurate to two decimal places. If we were to add the two masses together (one from each balance) we would be wrong to report our answer to four decimal places since our least accurate measurement is not that good.

First let's learn how to count significant figures in individual numbers and then we'll learn the rules for working with them.

   A. All non-zero digits are significant, unless otherwise indicated (meaning they come after an underline). *Note: We use underlines to keep track of significant figures when carrying out longer calculations.*

       3.45   3 significant figures

       3.4̲5   2 significant figures (the 3 and 4 are significant, the 5 is not)

B. Zeros are sometimes significant, depending on their location.

   a. **Leading zeros** appear *before* non-zero digits. These are not significant figures, only placeholders.

       0.0004   1 significant figure (the 4)

   b. **Captive zeros** appear *between* non-zero digits. These are always significant.

       3.05   3 significant figures

   c. **Trailing zeros** appear at the right end of a number. These are significant only if the number contains a decimal point, or if the significant figure is otherwise indicated (by being underlined). Trailing zeros in a number without a decimal point are placeholders.

       0.400   3 significant figures (the 4 and the two trailing zeros)

       4.0   2 significant figures

40,000	1 significant figures (only the 4)
40,000.	5 significant figures (all are significant)
4.00×10^4	3 significant figures
40,0<u>0</u>0	4 significant figures (all but the final zero are significant)

C. **Exact numbers** that determined by *counting* or by *definition* are considered to have infinite significant figures – they will not limit the significant figures in a calculation. some examples of exact numbers are:

2.54 centimeters in an inch

12 eggs in a dozen

33 people in a room

Since there is a limit to the accuracy of measured values, there must also be a limit to the accuracy of calculations performed using measured values. In general, we can say that a calculated value can be no more accurate than the least accurate measurement used in the calculation. However, exactly how the least-accurate measurement determines the number of significant figures in the calculated result depends on the operation performed.

Rules for Mathematical Operations

A. **Multiplication/Division**: The result of a multiplication or division operation must have the same number of *significant figures* as the measurement with the *fewest* number of significant figures.

Example: What is the area of a room with walls that measure 3.55 m by 11.65 m?

Area = length x width = (3.55 m)x(11.65m)

Entering this operation into a calculator gives *41.3585 m²*, but this answer implies a much more accurate answer than is possible. Since our measurement of 3.55 m only has three significant figures, so must our answer. We round our calculator answer to give three significant figures: **41.4 m²**.

B. Addition/Subtraction: The result of an addition or subtraction operation mist have the same number of *decimal places* as the measurement with the *fewest* number of decimal places. If the number doesn't have a decimal in it, then the result of the calculation cannot be more accurate than the last significant place (For example, 4<u>3</u>00 + 15.9 = 4<u>3</u>15.9 which becomes 4<u>3</u>00.)

Example: What is the perimeter of a room with walls that measure 3.55 m by 11.65 m?

Perimeter = length + length + width + width = 3.55m + 3.55m + 11.65m + 11.65m

Entering this operation into a calculator gives *30.4 m*, but this answer implies a less accurate answer than is our measurements. Since our measurements of 3.55 m and 11.65 m have two decimal places, so must our answer. We add a zero to our calculator answer to give a total of four significant figures: **30.40 m**.

Note: It's important to only round answers at the very end, not at every step.

1.1. Give the answer with the correct number of significant figures for the following:

a) 0.004708 x 0.050 = _____

b) 15.004 – 0.0009 = _____

c) 2.0270/10.3333 = _____

d) (3.4 + 1.13)/0.00874 = _____

Part 2: Scientific Notation

Scientific notation is a very convenient way of expressing very large or very small numbers in terms of "powers of 10". Numbers are expressed as **N x 10^x** where N is a number between 1 and 10 and x is an exponent – a power of 10.

$6,000,000 = 6 \times 10^6$ $0.06 = 6 \times 10^{-2}$

$600 = 6 \times 10^2$ $0.000000006 = 6 \times 10^{-9}$

To convert a number to scientific notation...

    1. Move the decimal point to the right or left to get a coefficient that is between 1 and 10.

    2. Count the spaces you moved the decimal place – this becomes the exponent on the 10.

      a) If you moved the decimal to the left, the exponent is positive.

      b) If you moved the decimal to the right, the exponent is negative.

Example: Write 3,492 in scientific notation. 3.492×10^3

Example: Write 0.08302 in scientific notation. 8.302×10^{-2}

2.1. Convert the following to scientific notation:

    a) 123,876.3 _____

    b) 42.2 _____

    c) 0.00023893 _____

    d) 9100 _____

2.2. Convert the following to standard notation:

    a) 3.6×10^{-5} _____

    b) 2.12×10^5 _____

    c) 4.8×10^{-8} _____

    d) 6.49×10^1 _____

2.3. In the following pairs, circle the *larger* number:

    a) 4.9×10^{-3} or 5.5×10^{-9}

    b) 1250   or 3.4×10^2

    c) 0.0000004   or 5×10^{-8}

    d) 9.08×10^{-6} or 7.4×10^6

Part 3: Measurement and Units

All physical measurements consist of a number and a unit. No measurement is complete without units. The unit tells you what kind of measurement was made: length, volume, mass, time, temperature, etc. There are many systems of units. In science, we typically use the metric or the SI (International System) system of units because they are based on the decimal system.

MEASUREMENT	METRIC	SI	OTHER UNITS
LENGTH	meter (m)	meter (m)	foot (ft), inch(in)
VOLUME	liter (L)	cubic meter (m³)	gallon (gal), ounce (oz)
MASS	gram (g), kilogram (kg)	kilogram (kg)	pound (lb), ounce (oz)
TIME	second (s)	second (s)	hour (hr), minute (min)
TEMPERATURE	Celsius (°C)	Kelvin (K)	Fahrenheit (°F)

3.1. Among the following choices, identify (circle) the measurement that has the SI unit.

a) John's height is:

      a. 1.5 yd   b. 6 ft   c. 2.1 m

b) The race was won in:

      a. 19.6 s   b. 14.2 min   c. 3.5 hr

c) The mass of the lemon is:

      a. 12 oz   b. 0.145 kg   c. 0.62 lb

d) The temperature is:

      a. 85 °C   b. 255 K   c. 45 °F

We use metric unit prefixes to express units in more manageable unit. A metric unit name consists of a base unit and a prefix to indicate the power of 10.

Examples:

      1 megaunit = 1,000,000 units = 10^6 units

      1 kilounit =   1,000 units = 10^3 units

      1 centiunit = 1/100 units = 0.01 units = 10^{-2} units

      1 milliunit =   1/1,000 units = 0.001 units = 10^{-3} units

Common metric prefixes:

PREFIX	SYMBOL	NUMERICAL VALUE	SCIENTIFIC NOTATION	EQUALITY
PETA	P	1,000,000,000,000,000	10^{15}	1 Pg = 10^{15} g
TERA	T	1,000,000,000,000	10^{12}	1 Tg = 10^{12} g
GIGA	G	1,000,000,000	10^{9}	1 Gm = 10^{9} m
MEGA	M	1,000,000	10^{6}	1 Mg = 10^{6} g
KILO	k	1,000	10^{3}	1 km = 10^{3} m
DECI	d	0.1	10^{-1}	1 dL = 10^{-1} L
				1 L = 10 dL
CENTI	c	0.01	10^{-2}	1 cm = 10^{-2} m
				1 m = 100 cm
MILLI	m	0.001	10^{-3}	1 mg = 10^{-3} g
				1 g = 1000 mg
MICRO	m	0.000001	10^{-6}	1 mg = 10^{-6} g
				1 g = 10^{6} mg
NANO	n	0.000000001	10^{-9}	1 nm = 10^{-9} m
				1 m = 10^{9} nm
PICO	p	0.000000000001	10^{-12}	1 ps = 10^{-12} s
FEMTO	f	0.000000000000001	10^{-15}	1 fs = 10^{-15} s

3.2. Complete the following metric relationships:

a) 1 kg = _____ g   1 g = _____ kg

b) 1 L = _____ cL   1 cL = _____ L

c) 1 Mm = _____ m   1 m = _____ Mm

3.3. In the following pairs, circle the *smaller* unit.

a) mg or g   b) µm or mm   c) kg or mg

Part 4: Conversion Factors and Dimensional Analysis

It is often necessary to convert a physical measurement from one system of units to a different system.

Unit equalities can be written as unit conversion factors which allow you to express a measurement in a different set of units.

For example, to convert between feet and miles, you can use the equality 5280 ft. = 1 mi. to create to conversion factors:

$$\frac{5280\ ft}{1\ mi} = 1 \quad and \quad \frac{1\ mi}{5280\ ft} = 1$$

This conversion factor can then be used to convert any amount of feet or miles into the other unit.

How many feet are in 1.500 miles?

$$1.500\ mi\ \left(\frac{5280\ ft}{1\ mi}\right) = 7920\ ft$$

Notice that the mile units cancel each other out (one in the numerator, one in the denominator) leaving only the units of feet in our final answer.

4.1. An iron sample has a mass of 4.50 lb. What is the mass of this sample in grams? (1 kg = 2.2046 lbs.; 1 kg = 1000g)

Practice Problems

1. Complete the following calculations to the appropriate number of sig. figs.:

        a) 234.52 + 25.2   = _____

        b) 1420 x 320.   = _____

        c) 529 ÷ 1.30   = _____

        d) 430. - 44.67   = _____

2. You take 20.4 mL of water from a graduated cylinder and add it to the beaker of water below. What is the new volume of water in the beaker?

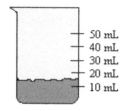

50 mL
40 mL
30 mL
20 mL
10 mL

3. A student finds that the weight of an empty beaker is 14.049 g. She places a solid in the beaker to give a combined mass of 14.142 g. To how many significant figures is the mass of the solid known?

4. The result of the following calculation has how many significant figures?

$$(0.4333 \text{ J/g } °C) (33.12°C - 31.12°C)(412.1 \text{ g})$$

Unit 2

Quantum Mechanics and the Atom

Part 1: Electromagnetic Radiation and the Bohr Model of the Atom

Electromagnetic Radiation and Light

Warm-Up Exercises

1.1. Sketch a wave. Show on the wave the parts related to frequency and wavelength.

1.2. Three waves are given below:

A.

B.

C.

a) Rank them in order of increasing frequency.

b) Rank them in order of increasing wavelength.

c) Rank them in order of increasing energy.

1.3. Arrange the following types of electromagnetic radiation in order of increasing wavelength: visible, X-ray, infrared.

Light is a type of electromagnetic radiation and is part of a broader spectrum of the EM spectrum that includes gamma rays, x-rays, UV, visible and infrared light, as well as microwaves and radio waves. These waves have characteristic frequencies and wavelengths that correspond to their energy. All electromagnetic radiation travels at the speed of light (known as the constant c = 3.0 x 10⁸ m/s). We can use the following two mathematical relationships to interconvert between wavelength (λ), frequency (ν), and Energy (E):

$$\lambda \cdot v = c$$

$$E = h \cdot v = \frac{h \cdot c}{\lambda}$$

where h = Planck's constant = 6.626 x 10⁻³⁴ J·s

1.4 Convert 500nm to m.

1.5 Electromagnetic radiation with the wavelength of 500 nm falls within which region of the spectrum?

1.6 What is the energy of a photon of wavelength 500 nm?

Light demonstrates properties that are consistent with being a wave, but also properties consistent with being a particle. When light waves interact they create interference patterns due to constructive and destructive interference. Furthermore, when light waves encounter a small opening, they bend around it. These are wave-like properties as we would expect from light waves. What many scientists found initially confusing was that light also displays particle-like properties as well. In the photoelectric effect, only light of a certain frequency was able to eject and electron from the surface of a metal. If light were simply a wave, this electron ejection should be observed at any frequency, given enough amplitude. That is not what was observed – a threshold *frequency* was required to eject the electron. This demonstrated the particle-like behavior of light. A simplistic way to think about light is that it comes in wave-like packets (called photons) that behave like particles or like waves depending on the circumstances.

1.7 Show the resulting wave if the following two waves are added together. Is this constructive or destructive interference?

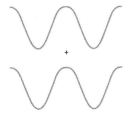

1.8 Show the resulting wave if the following two waves are added together. Is this constructive or destructive interference?

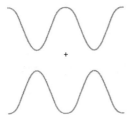

1.9 If the wavelength of light required to eject an electron from a particular metal is 400. nm, what will we observe in the following cases?

   a) We shine light with wavelength of 632 nm on the metal.

   b) We shine light with wavelength of 250. nm on the metal.

   c) We shine the same light as in part (b), but double the intensity.

How does this relate to atoms? When an element is heated to a sufficient temperature, it emits light. The light that is emitted is NOT a constant rainbow of light, however, it is a discrete pattern of lines, unique to each element. In fact, we can use these lines like a fingerprint to identify elements in unknown samples. How can we explain these lines and the source of light from elements? Let's explore our model of the atom to see how light and matter are connected.

Subatomic Particles and the Atom

Warm-Up Exercises

1.10. Sketch a simple diagram of an atom and label the parts (protons, neutrons, electrons). Describe the roles of each sub-atomic particle.

1.11. Fill in the missing information in the following table of <u>neutral atoms</u>:

Symbol	^{27}Al				
Element Name		Molybdenum	*Tungsten*	Uranium	
# Protons	13		74		
# Neutrons		56			
# Electrons					26
Mass number			182	238	58

1.12. Fill in the missing information in the following table of <u>ions</u>:

Symbol			$^{137}Ba^{2+}$		
Element Name		Zinc			Phosphorus
# Protons	16		56	40	
# Neutrons	16	34			
# Electrons				36	
Mass number	32		137	90	31
Charge	2-	2+	2+		3-

The Bohr Model and Atomic Emission

Bohr proposed that the emission of light when an element is heated comes from the movement of electrons between different energy levels. More specifically, he stated that electrons circled the nucleus in only certain allowed circular orbits. When an element is heated, the energy moves an electron into a higher orbit. When the electron falls to a lower energy level, light is emitted with exactly the energy of the difference in energy levels.

We can use the Bohr model to predict ΔE for any two energy levels in the hydrogen atom:

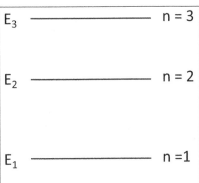

$$\Delta E = -2.178 \times 10^{-18} J \left(\frac{1}{n_{final}^2} - \frac{1}{n_{initial}^2} \right)$$

Note: As a rule, we use a **negative** sign for ΔE when energy is **emitted** and a **positive** sign for when it is **absorbed**.

1.13 According to the following energy diagram for the Bohr model of the hydrogen atom, if an electron falls from E_3 to E_1, is energy emitted or absorbed?

1.14 Given the three energy levels shown, how many emissive transitions are there? Sketch them on the diagram.

E_3 ———————	n = 3
E_2 ———————	n = 2
E_1 ———————	n =1

1.15 One of the lines in the hydrogen atom spectrum has a wavelength of 486.1 nm. If this electron ends in the n=2 energy level, what energy level did it start in?

1.16 What amount of energy is required to move an electron from n=1 to n=∞? What wavelength of light does this correspond to? (Note: This is the energy required to completely remove an electron from the hydrogen atom).

Bohr's model proposed that the orbits of electrons are quantized – electrons can only move between the specific energy levels, they cannot exist in between the energy levels. It is the transitions between these levels that give rise to the emission or absorption of light.

While the Bohr model successfully described the line spectrum of hydrogen and other one-electron systems, it could not adequately describe the spectra of atoms with more than one electrons (this is not a very convenient model, since there are many atoms with more than one electron!). The model also required a deterministic path for the electron – the orbit – which presented its own challenges to traditional physics (why didn't the atom emit radiation as the electron orbited the nucleus?). The Bohr model was an important stepping stone to the model we now use to understand the atom: the quantum-mechanical view of the atom.

Part 2: The Quantum-Mechanical View of the Atom

Electrons as Waves

It was accepted early on that light behaved as a wave, so the particle-like nature of light was a novel insight for physicists in the early 1900's. Even more shocking, perhaps, was the finding that **matter** exhibited wave-like properties.

A single electron traveling through space has a wavelength that is associated with its kinetic energy: the faster it is moving the higher its energy, the shorter its wavelength. Louis de Broglie related the wavelength of an electron to its velocity through the formula:

$$\lambda = \frac{h}{mv}$$ (h is still Planck's constant)

2.1 What is the de Broglie wavelength of an electron traveling at 3 m/s ($m_{electron}$ = 9.12 x 10^{-31} kg)?

2.2 What is the de Broglie wavelength of an 80 kg student running across campus at 3 m/s?

Note: This answer is 24 orders of magnitude smaller than gamma rays (10^{-12} m)

As you can see, the wave-like nature of you has very little impact on the uncertainty of your position. The wave-like nature of an electron, however, has a big impact on how we can know where it is. We cannot simultaneously observe the wave-like nature of an electron (its velocity) and its particle-like nature (its position). This is the root of the uncertainty principle.

When it comes to understanding electrons within at atom, it is helpful to think of them as standing waves, with the position of the electron described as a probability within an *orbital*.

A standing wave is a wave that oscillates back and forth within a fixed space, rather than moving through space. A good mental image is a plucked guitar string. The string vibrates in a wave, but is fixed (constrained) at either end. In a standing wave, any points that have zero displacement (don't move) are called *nodes*. The fixed ends of our guitar string are nodes. As we increase the frequency of the standing wave, we also increase the number of nodes.

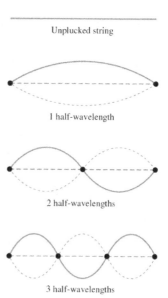

Unplucked string

1 half-wavelength

2 half-wavelengths

3 half-wavelengths

2.3 In the figure of standing waves at right, what happens to the following parts of the wave as the energy of the wave increases?

    a) Number of nodes?

    b) Frequency?

    c) Wavelength?

An electron wave can be thought of as a standing wave as well, but in three-dimensions. This is much harder to visualize. The electron wave is also constrained – by the interaction of the electron with the nucleus. The different standing wave patterns of an electron can be represented with mathematical functions called *wavefunctions*. The wavefunction (ψ) is a probability amplitude. The square of the wavefunction ($|\psi|^2$) is a probability density – where we'll find the largest amount of motion in a standing wave. The Schrödinger Equation describes the energies and wavefunctions available to the electron when it constrained by the atomic nucleus. In the hydrogen atom we use the probability density (the square of the wavefunction) to describe the region we are likely to find an electron. This is referred to as an "orbital".

There are multiple solutions to the Schrödinger Equation, yielding multiple orbitals. Each orbital is characterized by a set of quantum numbers (n, l, m_l).

2.4 Give a brief definition of the following quantum numbers. (Be sure to include their ranges, too.)

a) n

b) l

c) m_l

Quantum Numbers and Orbitals

The shapes of the orbitals are determined by their angular momentum quantum number (l).

For $l=0$ (s orbitals), orbitals are spherical. As n increases from 1 to 2 to 3, etc., the number of nodes increases. A node in an orbital is an area of zero electron density – an electron is not found there.

2.5 Sketch a cross-section for a 1s, 2s, and 3s orbital. Be sure to show any nodes present.

For $l=1$ (p orbitals), orbitals are "peanut shaped", with a node at the nucleus (the origin in a coordinate system). Since the magnetic quantum number (m_l) ranges from -1 to 1 for p orbitals, there are three orientations in space: along the x, y, and z axes.

2.6 Make four sketches, one for each of the $2p_x$, $2p_y$, and $2p_z$ orbitals and one in which all three of them are shown together all at once.

For $l=2$ (d orbitals) a wider variety of shapes are apparent. There are five total d orbitals (m_l = -2, -1, 0, 1, 2) and the labels of the d orbitals reflect the axes they occupy for the most part.

2.7 List the five d orbitals. How many nodes does each 3d orbital have?

2.8 Which of the following is NOT an allowed set of quantum numbers?

      A. n = 2, l = 1, m_l = -1

      B. n = 3, l = 0, m_l = 0

      C. n = 2, l = 2, m_l = -1

      D. n = 4, l = 2, m_l = 2

2.9 For the sets of quantum number, above, that are allowed, what type of orbital do they describe (i.e., 4s, 3d, etc.)?

There is one more quantum number we need to define and use. The spin magnetic quantum number (m_s) describes the "spin" of an electron: it can be "up" (m_s = +1/2, indicated with an up arrow ↑) or "down" (m_s = -+1/2, indicated with an down arrow ↓). We now have enough quantum numbers to describe the possible states on an electron in an atom.

Electron Configuration

In order to describe the configuration of electrons in an atom, we have a set of rules. The first rule is the **Pauli Exclusion Principle:** *No two electrons in an atom may occupy the same quantum state simultaneously – they cannot have the same set of quantum numbers.*

Practically, this means that each orbital can hold only two electrons: a spin-up electron, and a spin-down electron.

Our second rule is the **Aufbau Principle** (aufbua means "building up"): *Electrons fill the lowest energy orbitals first.* This means, we start at the bottom (in terms of energy), putting at most two electrons in that orbital before filling electrons into higher energy orbitals. In an atom with more than one electron (that's most of them!) we fill orbitals in this order: 1s, 2s, 2p, 3s, 3p, 4s, 3d, 4p, 5s, 4d, 5p, etc.

2.10 Show the electron configuration of the first four elements by filling in the spaces below with the correct number and orientation of arrows.

a) Hydrogen: ——
    1s

b) Helium: ——
    1s

c) Lithium: ——   ——
    1s   2s

d) Beryllium: ——   ——
    1s   2s

As we move to fill orbitals for the fifth element, we find the need for one more rule. How do we go about filling the three *p* orbitals? **Hund's Rule** guides us here: *The lowest energy configuration is one is which the maximum number of unpaired electron with parallel spin are distributed amongst a set of degenerate orbitals.* There's a lot of vocabulary in that rule: "degenerate orbitals" are orbitals with the same energy (such as the set of $2p_x$, $2p_y$, and $2p_z$ orbitals); "maximum number of unpaired electrons" means we prefer to put the electrons in their own orbital before we start pairing them up; "parallel spin" means we put those electrons into their orbitals with spins up.

2.11 Which of the following illustrations shows how three electrons in the 2p orbitals should be arranged according to Hund's Rule?

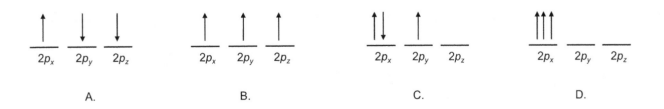

↑	↓	↓		↑	↑	↑		↑↓	↑		↑↑↑		
$2p_x$	$2p_y$	$2p_z$		$2p_x$	$2p_y$	$2p_z$		$2p_x$	$2p_y$	$2p_z$		$2p_x$	$2p_y$	$2p_z$
	A.				B.				C.				D.	

2.12 In the boron atom, what is the set of quantum numbers for the highest energy electron?

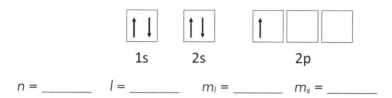

$n =$ _____ $l =$ _____ $m_l =$ _____ $m_s =$ _____

We can indicate the electron configuration in a more concise way than drawing boxes and arrows. For the boron atom shown above, we can write: $1s^2 2s^2 2p^1$ to indicate two electrons in the 1s orbital ($1s^2$), 2 electrons in the 2s orbital ($2s^2$), and one electron in the 2p orbitals ($2p^1$).

2.13 Fill in the orbital diagram and give the electron configuration ($1s^2 2s^2$, etc.) for oxygen.

Electron configuration: _____

The valence shell of an atom consists of the s and p orbitals in the highest-occupied n-level. In the cases of boron and oxygen, for example, the valence shell would be the 2s and 2p orbitals. We refer to *valence electrons* as the electrons in the valence shell.

2.14 How many valence electrons do the following elements have?

a) boron: _____   b) oxygen: _____   c) fluorine: _____   d) neon: _____

Part 3: The Periodic Table and Periodic Trends

The Periodic Table

Warm-Up Exercises

3.1. The elements can be classified as metals, non-metals, and metalloids. Create a rough sketch of the periodic table and show where each type of element is located, approximately.

3.2. Most elements occur as single atoms, but there are seven elements that occur as diatomic molecules in their elemental state. What are those seven elements?

3.3. List the elements that occur as gases at room temperature.

3.4. Elements in the same column tend to have similar properties. How many valence electrons do the following "families" have?

a) alkali metals: _____

b) alkaline earth metals: _____

c) halogens: _____

d) noble gases: _____

3.5. For the same families listed above, how many electrons do those elements need to gain or lose to achieve a noble gas electron configuration? (Circle gain or lose)

a) alkali metals: (gain/lose?) _____

b) alkaline earth metals: (gain/lose?)_____

c) halogens: (gain/lose?)_____

d) noble gases: (gain/lose?) _____

Periodic Trends

Since the periodic table is arranged in a way that groups elements into families with the same number of valence electrons, we can observe a variety of trends as we move through the table. We'll explore three general trends here:

Ionization Energy

> **Ionization energy is the energy required to remove an electron from an atom.**
>
> 3.6 Looking over the periodic table and thinking about stable electron configurations (think: noble gases), which family of elements would you expect be the easiest to remove an electron from?
>
> 3.7 Which family would be the hardest to remove an electron from?
>
> 3.8 As you move down a column of elements, the valence electrons tend to be further from the nucleus (and shielded from the protons by other electrons). Would you expect it to be easier or harder to remove an electron from an atom near the bottom of the periodic table compared to one in the same column, but near the top?
>
> 3.9 Sketch the periodic table and draw an arrow to indicate the general trend for "ease of ionization".

Electron Affinity

> **Electron affinity is the energy change associated with the addition of an electron to an atom or ion.** Electron affinity values are often expressed as negative values as a measure of the energy *released* (a negative sign indicates energy flows out) while forming a more stable species.
>
> 3.10 Which family of elements would achieve a noble gas configuration by accepting an additional electron?

3.11 Which elements would likely have positive (unfavorable) electron affinity values?

3.12 Sketch the periodic table and draw an arrow to indicate the general trend for "electron affinity".

Atomic Radius

The atomic radius of an element is determined in a variety of ways, but is helpful in describing the **general size of a neutral atom**.

3.13 Summarize the major influence on atomic radius as you move across a period of elements.

3.14 Summarize the major influence on atomic radius as you move down a column of the periodic table.

3.15 Sketch the periodic table and draw an arrow to indicate the general trend for "atomic radius".

Concept Mapping

A concept map is an important and useful way to create connection between the concepts you are learning in chemistry (and any other subject!). You start by choosing an overarching concept and then break that concept down into smaller parts, using arrows and linking words to show how ideas are connected. Learning requires that you create context around the ideas that are new to you. A concept map is one way to create that context.

Concept maps have the following characteristics:

1. They include a number of different concepts and show the relationships between the concepts.

2. They are a hierarchical arrangement of concepts which show degrees of generality and inclusiveness. The concepts found at the top of the map are the most general and will include the concepts which are found further down in the concept map.

3. Concepts are placed inside of circles, rectangles or ellipses.

4. Concepts are linked by **LINKING WORDS**. Linking words are usually verbs, verb phrases, adverbs, or prepositions. When the concepts plus their linking words are read together, they form a proposition.

5. There are also **CROSS-LINKAGES** in concept maps. These occur horizontally between concepts in the map. The best concept maps will always have both links and cross-links.

6. Under each of the lowest level concepts we might also list specific examples for those concepts.

NOTE: Examples are not enclosed in a circle, rectangle, or ellipse.

Some things to remember that will help get you started:

1. Practice is the key to good concept mapping.

2. A concept map does not have to be symmetrical. It can more concepts on the right side than on the left, or *vice versa*.

3. Remember that a concept map is a short cut way of representing information. Do not try to include every last detail, but include enough that you can make sense of the main ideas.

4. Do not expect one person's map to be exactly like another's map. Everyone thinks a little differently and may see different relationships between certain concepts. Other's maps may appear in a different format although both yours and theirs may be correct.

5. At first, mapping is time consuming, but it becomes easier and faster after your first few maps are made.

Characteristics of a good concept map:

Although there is no such thing as the 'right' concept map for a given topic, there are several characteristics that well-constructed maps have in common.

1. A concept map usually stems from one main idea.

2. The main idea branches into related general concepts.

3. General concepts can be subdivided into more specific concepts branching from them in several tiers.

4. Specific concepts are elaborated by example.

5. Concepts are usually nouns, representing objects or events. *Each concept* should be a single idea and *appear only once in the map.*

6. Relationships between concepts are shown by linking words (usually verb, verb phrases, adverbs, or prepositions). **ALL** concepts should be linked.

7. Cross-linkages are used to connect concepts in two different paths of the map. The more cross-linkages, the better, since they demonstrate an increased depth of understanding. Lines for linkages may hop over each other.

8. Any two concepts and their linking word taken in isolation should form a <u>complete</u> thought.

Create a concept map for the previous material using the following key words (you may add more!):

atom	proton	neutron	electron	energy level	transition	emission
wavelength	frequency	electromagnetic radiation	light	photon	wave	absorption
wave equation	probability	quantum numbers	electron configuration	orbital	quantized	node
ionization energy	electron affinity	valence electrons	atomic radius	valence shell	energy	spectrum

Unit 3

Chemical Bonding

Part 1: Bonding and Lewis Dot Structures

Representing Compounds

Warm-Up Exercises

1.1. Classify the following models as atom, diatomic element, compound, or mixture.

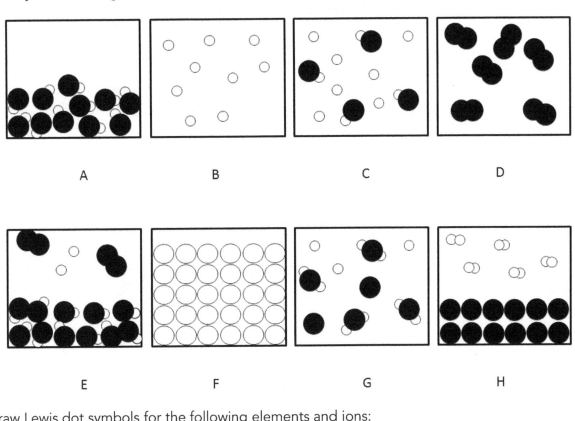

1.2. Draw Lewis dot symbols for the following elements and ions:

    a) Br   b) Cl⁻   c) N   d) Ar

    e) Na^+ f) O^{2-} g) Mg^{2+} h) H

1.3. Which of the atoms/ion above have full valence shells?

Chemical Bonding

Chemical bonds can be classified into two major categories: ionic bonds and covalent bonds.

Ionic Bonds

An ionic bond is a bond that holds species of opposite charge together. Generally, ionic bonds occur between a metal (which loses electrons) and a non-metal (which gains electrons). The classic example of an ionic compound is sodium chloride (NaCl, table salt). The positively charged sodium ions (Na^+) and the negatively charged chloride ions (Cl^-) are held together by electrostatic attraction.

1.4 For each of the pairs of neutral elements below, predict how they would lose/gain electrons to form ionic compounds. The first one is done for you as an example. Remember that your overall compound should be neutral, so it's ok to add more of one type of ion as necessary.

a) K and Br

K would lose one electron to form K^+, Br would gain one electron to form Br^-. Together they form the ionic compound KBr.

b) Li and F

c) Mg and Cl

d) Ca and O

e) Na and O

Covalent bonds

Covalent bonds involve the sharing of electron in order for each atom to reach a full octet. Covalent bonds are usually formed between two non-metals. We depict the covalent bonds in these molecules using Lewis dot structures – a type of model for depicting what molecules look like. There are three general steps for creating a simple Lewis dot structure:

1. Add up all of the valence electrons from each of the elements in the molecule. This is the total number of electrons you will have to work with.

2. Use pairs of electron to form a bond between each of the atoms in your molecule.

3. Arrange the remaining electrons around the atoms as either lone pairs (pairs of electrons NOT involved in a bond) or additional bonds until every atom in the molecule has a full valence shell (eight electrons – a full octet – or two electrons for H and He).

The easier way to learn is to try a few.

1.5 Let's build a Lewis dot structure for NO_2^-.

a) How many total valence electrons will we use in our Lewis dot structure? (Note: This molecule has a negative charge, which adds one additional electron).

b) Use the following template to assemble your Lewis dot structure:

$$O \quad N \quad O$$

Use four of your total electrons to create two bonds – one each between the N and each O. Use the remaining electrons to make sure each atom has eight electrons around them, counting bonds as two electrons for each atom they are connected to. Be sure to use the exact number of electron you counted in part a).

Since the molecule has an overall negative charge, add a square bracket and a negative sign to the finished molecule.

1.6 Which of the following is a correct Lewis dot structure for NO_2^-?

1.7 For the structures above that are NOT correct, describe why they are incorrect.

Electronegativity and Polarity

Warm-Up Exercises

1.8. Sketch a diagram of the periodic table and draw an arrow to indicate the overall trend in electronegativity.

1.9. Rank the following elements in order of increasing electronegativity: Sr, Cs, Se, O.

1.10. Rank the following bonds in order of **increasing** ionic character: S-F, Se-F, O-F.

1.11. Draw the dipole moment in the following bonds (you may want to consult a table of electronegativity values in your textbook):

a) C-O

b) I-Cl

c) Br-N

d) B-H

A Deeper Look at Lewis Dot Structures: Resonance, Formal Charge, Octet Exceptions

Lewis dot structures are simple models for molecular bonding. Sometimes, however, there might be more than one way to create a valid structure using the rules we have outlined. How can we judge which structure is "most valid"?

First we have to take into account that Lewis dot structures can be drawn in multiple, fully equivalent ways. For example, the two possible structures we can draw for ozone (O_3) are functionally identical: they consist of one O-O double bond and one O-O single bond:

$$\ddot{O}=\ddot{O}-\ddot{O}: \qquad :\ddot{O}-\ddot{O}=\ddot{O}$$

Unless we could distinguish one oxygen atom from the other, we would have no way to tell these apart. In reality, however, the ozone molecule has been found to have two identical O-O bonds. Here is where our Lewis dot model starts to break down a little. So, we expand our model slightly to include the idea of "resonance structures" – structures that differ only in the position of multiple bonds and lone pairs. both of the structures, above, are resonance structures for ozone and the "real structure of ozone is an average of those two structures, where the double bond is "spread out" across all of the oxygen atoms:

$$\ddot{O}=\ddot{O}-\ddot{O}: \longleftrightarrow :\ddot{O}-\ddot{O}=\ddot{O} \quad \Longrightarrow \quad O\text{----}O\text{----}O$$

When drawing Lewis dot structures we try to draw all of the resonance structures so we can develop a clearer picture of the molecule "in real life".

1.12 Draw all the possible resonance structures for N_3^-. Remember to use the correct number of total electrons and to give each atom a complete octet.

Not all resonance structures contribute the same "weight" to the correct picture of a molecule. In order to judge if a certain resonance structure is "better" than another, we need to add one more procedure.

1.13 Draw two valid Lewis dot structures for NCS^-.

N   C   S   N   C   S

In order to judge if one structure is more correct than the other, we need to assign formal charges. Assigning formal charges is just an electron accounting procedure used to determine the most likely Lewis dot structure from several options.

When finding the formal charge for an atom we compare the number of valence electron it typically has to the number of electron it has around it in the structure. We count electrons in a slightly different way for the second part – counting only one electron in a bond. For example, in the molecule HF:

$$H\!\!-\!\!\ddot{\underset{\cdot\cdot}{F}}:$$

- H has one electron assigned to it (from the bond with F)
- F has seven electrons assigned to it (one from the bond with H and 6 lone pair electrons)

We compare these numbers to the typical valence electrons that H and F have. H has one valence electron and F has seven, so both of these atoms have no net formal charge in the molecule.

Now let's look at NCS⁻.

1.14 How many valence electrons do N, C and S usually have?

N: _____   C: _____   S: _____

1.15 In the following two structures, how many electron do N, C, and S have around them? Compare that number to the number of valence electrons in the previous question and fill in the blanks with the formal charge for each atom (+1 if the atom has fewer electrons around it than valence electrons, 0 if the number of electrons is the same, -1 if the number of electrons is one more than the valence electrons and so on).

N: _____ C: _____ S: _____   N: _____ C: _____ S: _____

The "best" structure is the one in which the individual formal charges have the lowest magnitudes. If two structures have the same magnitude of formal charges, the best structure has the negative charge on the most electronegative atom.

1.9 Which of the following structures for NCS⁻ is most correct? Assign formal charges to each atom in all the structures.

A   B   C   D

1.16 Draw three possible structures for CO_2. Which one is the most correct?

Some molecules can (and regularly do) violate the octet rule. There are two types of violations to consider: sub-octet systems (less than 8 electrons) and valence shell expansion.

Sub-Octet Systems

Some atoms (not many) can form stable molecules that do not fulfill the octet rule. Specifically, these are Be, B, and Al. Since Be and Al are typically involved in ionic bonding, boron is the primary sub-octet atom we see the most. In drawing Lewis dot structures involving boron, it is typically more acceptable to leave boron with an incomplete octet than to create double bonds.

Valence Shell Expansion

For third-row elements (and beyond) occasionally exhibit expanded octets up to 12 or 14 total electrons. This is not so much a violation of the octet rule, but an example of an atom using additional orbitals. In first-row elements (H, and He) we are limited to two electrons (the duet rule) because only two electrons can fill the 1s orbital. When we move to the second row, we can have eight electrons filling the 2s and 2p orbitals. When we move to the 3rd period, however, we gain access to the d-orbitals, offering up to 10 more spaces for electrons – a total of 18 electrons can be held in the 3s, 3p, and 3d orbitals. We rarely need to (or are able to because of space constraints) arrange 18 electrons around an atom, but in molecules like SF_6, it is clear that we must have more than eight electrons around our central sulfur atom.

1.17 Draw two possible Lewis dot structure for I_3^-. Which one is "more correct" according to formal charge?

Bond Length and Strength

One of the main pieces of evidence we have for resonance structures is measurements of bond lengths and strengths in molecules. For example, in our model of ozone we developed two possible resonance structures:

$$\overset{..}{O} = O - \overset{..}{\underset{..}{O}} : \qquad : \overset{..}{\underset{..}{O}} - O = \overset{..}{O}$$

A typical O-O bond length (single) is about 148 pm. The typical O=O bond length (double) is 121 pm. When the bond lengths or ozone are measured we find they have a bond length of 128 pm – slightly longer than a double bond, but shorter than a single bond. Additionally, both O-O bonds are the same length – one is not longer than the other. This is good evidence that the actual structure of ozone is essentially an average of the two resonance structures. Similarly, the strength of the bonds in ozone are about 1.5 that of an O-O single bond: slightly stronger, but not as strong as a double bond.

There are two general trends related to bonds and their strength and length: Multiple bonds tend to be stronger than single bonds and multiple bonds tend to be shorter than single bonds.

The strength of bonds can be measured using **bond enthalpy** (or bond energy): the amount of energy need to break one mole of a bond in the gas phase.

A chemical reaction involves breaking bonds in reactant molecules and making bonds in the product molecules. We can use the bond enthalpies for our reactant and product molecules to estimate the amount of energy a reaction will require or release. This value is called $\Delta H°_{rxn}$ and can be calculated in this way:

$$\Delta H_{rxn}° = \Sigma(\Delta H's\ of\ bonds\ broken) + \Sigma(\Delta H's\ of\ bonds\ formed)$$

Bond breaking is always a positive value (endothermic, requires energy).

Bond making is always a negative value (exothermic, releases energy).

If the overall sum is positive, the reaction requires energy (endothermic). If the overall sum is negative, the reaction releases energy (exothermic).

Bond	Bond Energy (kJ/mol)	Bond	Bond Energy (kJ/mol)	Bond	Bond Energy (kJ/mol)
H-H	436	C=C	611	N-N	163
H-C	414	C-N	305	N=N	418
H-N	389	C≡N	891	O-O	142
H-Cl	431	C-O	360	O=O	498
C-C	347	C=O	736	I-I	151

1.18 Use the data in the table above to determine how much energy is required to break all the bonds in the following molecules. (*Hint: You may need to draw the Lewis dot structures first*).

a) I_3^-

b) O_3

c) NH_3

d) HCN

1.19 For the following compounds: HCCH, H_2CCH_2, and H_3CCH_3...

  a) Rank the compounds in order of *increasing* carbon-carbon bond *strength*.

  b) Rank the compounds in order of *decreasing* carbon-carbon bond *length*.

Part 2: Molecules

Molecular Compounds

Warm-Up Exercises

2.1. Give the names for the following molecules and compounds:

a) $MgCl_2$ _____   b) Na_2O _____

c) KBr _____   d) Ca_3N_2 _____

e) N_2O_5 _____   f) CCl_4 _____

g) SO_2 _____   h) S_2Br_2 _____

2.2. In the problem above, circle the ionic compounds.

2.3. Draw the Lewis dot structures for the following covalent compounds. (The central atom is underlined.)

a) $\underline{C}O_2$ b) $H_2\underline{C}O$ c) O_3

d) <u>carbon</u> tetrachloride   e) <u>phosphorous</u> trichloride   f) water

Molecular shape

Lewis dot structures help us assemble molecules from the formula, but they don't really tell us what the molecule looks like in three dimensions. We can use what we know about Lewis dot structures and the types of electrons in them to develop a model for the three-dimensional shape of molecules. This model is valence-shell electron-pair repulsion (VSEPR).

The main premise behind VSEPR is that electron repel each other and by doing so spread out as far from each other as possible in a molecule. This gives rise to a few distinctive shapes that atoms can adopt in terms of how they form bonds with other atoms.

This flowchart can help you find the three-dimensional shape of simple molecules:

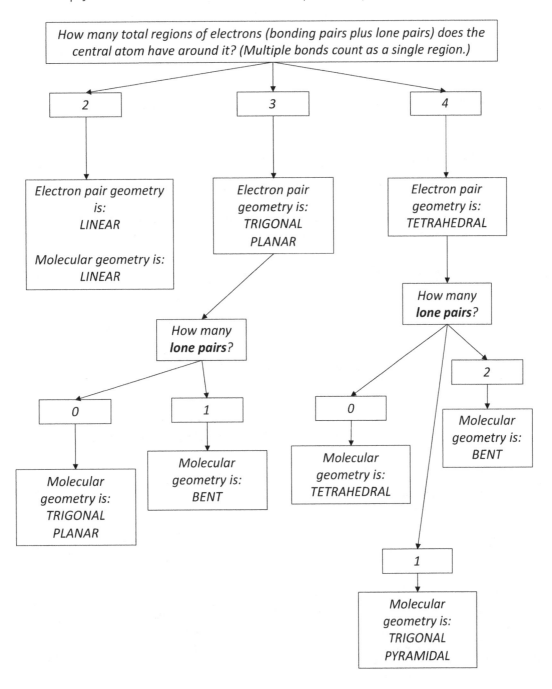

2.4 Using the Lewis dot structures you drew in the #3 of the Warm-Up Exercises, give the electron pair geometry and the molecular geometry for each of the molecules.

a) CO_2

electron pair geometry: _____ molecular geometry: _____

b) H_2CO

electron pair geometry: _____ molecular geometry: _____

c) O_3

electron pair geometry: _____ molecular geometry: _____

d) carbon tetrachloride

electron pair geometry: _____ molecular geometry: _____

e) phosphorous trichloride

electron pair geometry: _____ molecular geometry: _____

f) water

electron pair geometry: _____ molecular geometry: _____

If our molecule has more than four regions of electrons around it, we can use an expanded flowchart:

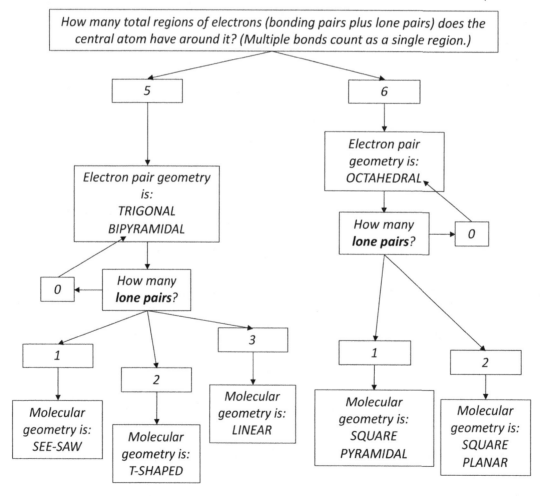

2.5 Give the electron-pair geometry and molecular geometry (shape) for the following compounds:

a) BrF_3

electron pair geometry: _____ molecular geometry: _____

b) ICl_4^-

electron pair geometry: _____ molecular geometry: _____

c) XeF_2

electron pair geometry: _____ molecular geometry: _____

d) BrF_5

electron pair geometry: _____ molecular geometry: _____

e) SCl_6

electron pair geometry: _____ molecular geometry: _____

Polarity in Molecules

Warm-Up Exercises

2.6. Sketch the sum of the following vectors:

a)

b)

c)

d)

e)

f)

We now have the ability to take many of the concepts we have studied (electronegativity, bonding, VSEPR, vector addition) and make predictions about whether or not a molecule will be *polar* – simply by knowing the formula! The polarity of molecules is important because it determines how the molecules will interact (or not) with other types of polar and non-polar molecules.

A polar molecules is a molecule with a **permanent dipole moment**. While many bonds are polar, the shape of the molecule determines whether or not those individual dipole moments cancel out or add together.

To determine if a molecules is polar, we follow a few simple steps that rely on our previous understanding:

    1. Draw the Lewis dot structure of the molecule.

    2. Determine the three-dimensional shape of the molecule using VSEPR.

    3. Identify any polar bonds in the molecule and sketch their individual dipole moments with an arrow.

    4. Use vector addition to determine if the individual dipole moments cancel each other out or create a permanent dipole moment. If they cancel, the molecule is non-polar. If they do not, it is polar.

2.7 Determine whether or not the following molecules are polar. (The central atoms are underlined.)

    a) $\underline{B}H_3$ b) $\underline{P}F_3$

    c) $\underline{N}O_2^-$ d) $\underline{S}Cl$

Polyatomic Ions and Naming Acids

Polyatomic ions are simply covalent compounds with an overall ionic charge. The can form ionic compounds with metals, but remain bonded together as a polyatomic ion when dissolved in water.

2.8 Draw Lewis dots structure (with any necessary resonance structures) for the following polyatomic ions.

    a) ammonium ion   b) nitrate ion

    c) sulfate ion   d) phosphate ion

    e) hydroxide ion   f) sulfite ion

2.9 Give the formulas for the following compounds.

a) sodium nitrate

b) aluminum hydroxide

c) ammonium carbonate

d) potassium phosphate

e) sodium cyanide

f) ammonium sulfate

2.10 Acids are often closely related to our common polyatomic ions. Give the formulas for each of the compounds listed.

a) nitric acid and nitrate ion

b) sulfuric acid and sulfate ion

c) phosphoric acid and phosphate ion

d) acetic acid and acetate ion

What atom(s) is (are) added to the polyatomic ions when they are in their acidic form? _____

Part 3: Valence Bond Theory and Hybridization

Using Lewis dot structures and VSEPR to predict the shape of molecules is very useful and is an amazingly accurate predictor of shape, despite the simplicity of the process. While these models are good at telling us *how* to predict the shape, they are not very good at telling us *why* we see what we see. This brings us to Valence Bond Theory and the Localized Electron Model. This model states that chemical bonds are created by the overlap (and blending) of atomic orbitals to form hybridized orbitals. This theory was important in explaining how the 2s and 2p orbitals of carbon could somehow create the tetrahedral geometry observed in carbon-containing molecules like methane (CH_4).

There are three main types of orbitals we'll study in the course: sp^3, sp^2 and sp hybrid orbitals.

3.1 The sp^3 orbital gives rise to tetrahedral geometry in atoms. Sketch a three-dimensional diagram of a sp^3 orbital.

3.2 The sp^2 orbital gives rise to the trigonal planar geometry of atoms with a double bond, leaving an unhybridized p orbital available to form the second bond with another atom.

a) Sketch a diagram of a sp^2 orbital.

b) Sketch a diagram of two sp^2 atoms near each other. Add (preferably in a different color) the unhybridized p orbital on each atom and show how they would interact to form a π-bond.

3.3 The sp orbital gives rise to the linear geometry of atoms with triple bonds, leaving two unhybridized p orbitals available to form additional bonds.

a) Sketch a diagram of a sp orbital.

b) Sketch a diagram of two sp atoms near each other. Add (preferably in two different colors) the unhybridized p orbitals on each atom and show how they would interact to form two π-bonds.

3.4 Give the hybridization of each carbon atom in the following molecules:

a)

b)

Part 4: Molecular Composition

Atomic and Molar Mass

Warm-Up Exercises

4.1. The atomic mass unit is a defined quantity. It is defined as 1/12 the mass of a carbon-12 atom. How many protons, neutrons and electron are in a carbon-12 atom?

4.2. The mass unit of 1 amu is equal to 1.66054×10^{-27} kg. A single carbon-12 atom weighs 12 amu. What is this mass in kg?

4.3. How many atoms of carbon-12 would it take to weigh exactly 12.000 g?

4.4. The number you found in the previous question is Avogadro's number and is simply a way to relate number of atoms to their mass in amu. If you have a particle that weighs 1 amu exactly, how many grams would 6.022×10^{23} of those particles weigh?

4.5. If you scooped up a handful of pure carbon, you would have a mixture of carbon-12 (98.9 %, weighing exactly 12 amu) and carbon-13 (1.1 %, weighing 13.003 amu). Why would 6.022×10^{23} of these particles not weigh exactly 12.000 g?

4.6. If you had 3.5 g of carbon (12.011 g/mol), how many atoms of carbon does this represent?

4.7. If you had one mole of carbon dioxide (CO_2) how many grams would it weigh?

Composition of Molecules

Molecules are too small for us to observe directly, so being able to understand what a molecule is made of is one of the classic problems confronting chemists. How do you know what you have? If you made a chemical, how do you know you did it correctly? The traditional approach to solving this type of problem was often to determine the substances composition through a number of techniques. One of those techniques still used today is called *elemental analysis*. In order to understand how to use and interpret the results of elemental analysis, it's important to learn a few key terms and ideas.

Mass fraction

> The mass fraction of part of a substance is the mass of a particular component (usually an element) divided by the mass of the entire substance. This is usually expressed as a percent.

4.1 One mole of water (H_2O) is made up of 2.016 g H and 16.00 g O with a total mass of 18.016 g. What is the mass fraction of H and O in water?

%H: %O:

4.2 Carbon dioxide (CO_2) has a molar mass of 44.011 g/mol. Carbon dioxide is 27.29% carbon. What is the mass fraction of oxygen in carbon dioxide?

Percent composition

> If we know the percent composition of a substance (that is the mass fraction of each component), we can determine a simple formula that gives the ratio of elements in the substance. Since we know how much elements weigh (thank you periodic table!), we can turn the percent composition of a substance back into formulas. There are two cases to consider: 1) we do not know the overall molar mass (common if you have a new or unknown substance) and 2) we know the overall molar mass (common if you are confirming that you made the right thing).

4.8 Assume to have 100 g of an unknown substance but you know that it is made of only Cl, C and H in the following amounts. Convert each of the percentages to grams and then to moles of each element.

89.10% Cl

10.05% C

0.85% H

4.9 In the previous problem, you now have the mole ratios of the three elements in the molecule. If you divide each mole amount by the smallest mole amount (making the smallest amount then equal to one), what is the ratio of chlorine : carbon : hydrogen that you find?

Empirical and Molecular Formulas

The simplest ratio of elements in a formula is known as the empirical formula. It represents the of elements with respect to each other, but it may not be the exact formula for the molecule you are studying. For example, a molecule with the empirical formula CH_2O could be actually CH_2O (formaldehyde) or $C_6H_{12}O_6$ (glucose). You would not want to confuse the two! In order to know the molecular formula we need the molar mass of the whole molecule.

4.10 The molar mass of the molecule in the previous question is found to be 119.349 g/mol. What is the formula for this substance?

4.11 If, instead, the molar mass was found to be 358.047 g/mol, what would the molecular formula be?

Elemental Analysis

Elemental analysis is the technique chemists use to verify the formula of the compound they have made or to help them understand what the formula might possibly be. The compound is burned in excess oxygen with the products of the combustion carefully weighed. A very precise starting mass is necessary for this calculation to be accurate.

The products of combustion can be used to calculate the percent composition of the substance, but require a few additional steps. For example, when a compound containing only C, H, and O is combusted via elemental analysis, the amount of carbon in the sample is determined by the amount of CO_2 produced. The amount of hydrogen is determined from the amount of water produced. How can we get the amount of oxygen in the sample?

4.12 One of the chemical substances that we associate with the smell of fresh orange juice is sent for elemental analysis. The compound contains only C, H, and O is combusted with excess oxygen gas. The original sample weighs 7.95 mg. The analysis gives 18.07 mg CO_2 ad 7.40 mg of H_2O. What masses of C, H, and O make up the original sample? (*Hint: Use the mass fraction of C in CO_2 to find the mass of carbon and the mass fraction of H in H_2O to find the mass of hydrogen. What mass remains unaccounted for compared to the original mass of the sample?*)

C: _____ mg   H: _____ mg   O: _____ mg

4.13 Now that you have the masses for C, H, and O, use the original mass of the sample (7.95 mg) to find the percent composition and the empirical formula of the substance.

C: _____ %   H: _____ %   O: _____ %   Empirical formula: _____

Concept Map

Create a concept map using the following key words. You may add any additional words, as necessary.

valence electrons	Lewis dot symbols	ionic bonds	cations	anions
covalent bonds	electronegativity	polarity	dipole moment	polar bonds
resonance	formal charge	octet	bond length	bond strength
VSEPR	repulsion	electron-pair geometry	molecular shape	vectors
hybridization	orbitals	lone pairs	bonding pairs	energy

Unit 4

Stoichiometry and Reactions

Part 1: Stoichiometry of Chemical Reactions

Writing and Balancing Chemical Equations

Warm-Up Exercises

1.1. Write a chemical equation for the following model:

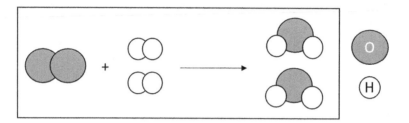

1.2. Briefly summarize the Law of Conservation of Mass. What does it mean for a chemical equation?

1.3. Convert the following sentence to a chemical equation, using the correct symbols. Be sure to include states of matter (solid, liquid, gas, etc.) and to balance your reaction.

Solid aluminum reacts with aqueous sulfuric acid to produce aqueous aluminum sulfate and hydrogen gas.

1.4. Convert the following chemical equation to words.

$$4 \, HCl \, (g) + O_2 \, (g) \rightarrow 2 \, H_2O \, (g) + 2 \, Cl_2 \, (g)$$

1.5. Balance the following reactions:

a) ____ C_6H_{14} (g) + ____ O_2 (g) → ____ CO_2 (g) + ____ H_2O (g)

b) ____ $Co(NO_3)_3$ (aq) + ____ $(NH_4)_2S$ (aq) → ____ Co_2S_3 (s) + ____ NH_4NO_3 (aq)

c) ____ FeS (s) + ____ HCl (aq) → ____ $FeCl_2$ (aq) + ____ H_2S (g)

Stoichiometry

As you have seen, we represent chemical reactions with chemical equations that convey a great deal of information: states of matter, reactants, products, ratios of substances relative to each other, etc. Stoichiometry is the numerical relationship between substances in a chemical reaction. For example, in the reaction

$$4 \text{ HCl (g)} + \text{O}_2 \text{ (g)} \rightarrow 2 \text{ H}_2\text{O (g)} + 2 \text{ Cl}_2 \text{ (g)}$$

the equation tells us we need four molecules of HCl for every one molecule of oxygen gas. It also tells us that our products will be two molecules of water for every two molecules of chlorine gas. The equation must be *balanced* for these ratios to be correct. Since these equations represent molecules, they can also be scaled up to represent moles of substances, too.

1.6 According to the reaction above, how many molecules of water will be produced for every four molecules of HCl?

1.7 According to the reaction above, how many molecules of water will be produced if we used eight molecules of HCl? (*Assume there is plenty of oxygen.*)

1.8 Still referring to the reaction above...

   a) Write a generic relationship (as a fraction, called a mole ratio) that relates moles of water to moles of HCl. Write is such that moles of water is on the top of your fraction.

   b) Use your mole ratio to find how many moles of water are produced from 3.7 moles of HCl.

1.9 Set up a new mole ratio and use it to show how many moles of chlorine gas would be produced by reacting 7.6 moles of HCl with plenty of oxygen.

Limiting Reactants

In the previous problems you worked, you may have noticed that the reactions had "plenty of oxygen". what happens when there isn't enough oxygen to react with all the HCl? When that happens, we say the amount of products is "limited" by the oxygen. We can't make the full amount because we have run out of ingredients in our recipe.

1.10 Using the balanced equation for the reaction of HCl and O₂ given on the previous page, draw a representation of the contents of the container below after the reaction has happened. Be sure to remember that the number of elements / particles must stay constant from the beginning to the end of the reaction (Law of Conservation of Mass).

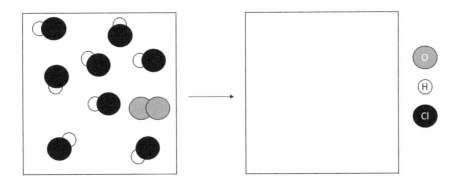

1.11 In the reaction 2A + 3B → C, when 4.0 moles of A are mixed with 4.0 moles of B, which reactant is limiting?

We can combine our knowledge of stoichiometry, mole ratios, and molar mass to work with gram amounts of reactants and predict gram amounts of products. This process requires a few steps:

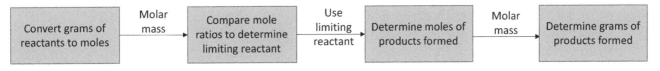

As you can see, though, each step is one we have done already: grams to moles, mole ratios, limiting reactant, moles to grams. Try it here:

1.12 Using our chemical reaction from earlier:

$$4 \text{ HCl (g)} + \text{O}_2 \text{ (g)} \rightarrow 2 \text{ H}_2\text{O (g)} + 2 \text{ Cl}_2 \text{ (g)}$$

A mixture of 72.9 g of HCl and 32.0 g of oxygen is allowed to react. How many grams each of water and chlorine gas are produced? How much unreacted product is left over?

Percent Yield

Now that we know how to predict how much we *should* produce in a reaction, we can compare it to how much we *actually* produce in a reaction in the lab. Many chemists will tell you that, sadly, these two numbers are rarely the same! Why don't we make exactly the same amount as we predicted? A number of reasons, such as: incomplete reaction, side-reactions that make different products, loss of product when we collect / purify it, etc. Most chemists will report the "percent yield" of a reaction to help others predict how to scale their reaction in order to make enough of what they need.

$$percent\ yield = \frac{actual\ yield}{theoretical\ (predicted)yield} \times 100\%$$

1.13 If, in the reaction you did in the previous question, you collected 10.2 g of water, what is the percent yield of your reaction?

Part 2: Solutions and Concentration

Calculating Concentration

Warm-up Exercises

2.1. Concentration is most commonly reported in units of molarity (M): moles/liter. What is the molarity of a solution that contains 0.3 mol of KNO_3 in 250 mL of water?

2.2. We can also express the concentration of individual ions in solution. For example, what is the concentration of chloride ions in a solution in which 0.2 mol of $MgCl_2$ is dissolved in 500 mL of water?

2.3. If you wanted to prepare 300. mL of a 1.50 M solution of NaCl, how many grams of NaCl would you need to weigh out?

2.4. How could you use your solution, above, to prepare 500 mL of a 0.3 M solution?

Electrolytes

Compounds that separate into ions when dissolved in water are called "electrolytes". Perhaps you have heard this term in ads for sports drinks. Ions are necessary for proper muscle functioning in your body, so replenishing the ions that you lose through sweat is important. A solution in which a large number of ions is present in water can conduct electricity. If no ions are present, electricity will not flow through the solution. We can classify three types of compounds based on how they form (or don't form) ions in water:

Strong Electrolytes

>   A strong electrolyte is an ionic compound or a strong acid that dissolves completely in water, creating many ions. For example, when NaCl is dissolved in water, the water molecules hydrate the ions, surrounding them and separating them from each other. These ions then move freely throughout the solution.

2.5 List some examples of strong electrolytes.

Weak Electrolytes

>   Week electrolytes form a few ions in solution. Usually a weak electrolyte is an ionic compound that is only slightly soluble in water (so not much of it is hydrated and separated by the water molecules) or a weak acid or base that does not generate many free H^+ of OH^- ions (more on these later). How do you know if an ionic compound will be soluble or not? Here are a few simple rules:

>>   1. If the compound contains an alkali earth metal ion (Li^+, Na^+, K^+, Cs^+, Rb^+), the nitrate ion (NO_3^-) or the ammonium ion (NH_4^+), it is most likely soluble.

>>   2. Ionic compounds containing chloride, bromide, and iodide ions are usually soluble, unless they contain the ions Ag^+ or Pb^{2+}.

>>   3. Sulfate (SO_4^{2-}) salts are usually soluble, except for $BaSO_4$, $PbSO_4$ and $CaSO_4$ which are all essentially insoluble.

>>   4. Hydroxide (OH^-) salts are not usually very soluble, unless they are paired with an ion in #1 above.

>>   5. Compounds containing sulfide (S^{2-}), carbonate (CO_3^{2-}), chromate (CrO_4^{2-}), and phosphate (PO_4^{3-}) are only slightly soluble.

2.6 List some examples of weak electrolytes.

Nonelectrolytes

A compound will not act as an electrolyte if it does not generate ions in solution. Covalent compounds do not separate into ions when dissolved in water - they remain intact and neutral. Likewise, insoluble ionic compounds do not form ions – they stick together as overall neutral ionic pairs.

2.7 List some examples of nonelectrolytes.

2.8 Predict whether the following solutions would be strong, weak, or nonelectrolyte solutions.

Compound	Strong, weak, or nonelectrolyte?
C_6H_{14}	
KBr	
$PbSO_4$	
NaOH	
$Ca_3(PO_4)_2$	
$PbCl_2$	
KNO_3	

Part 3: Types of Reactions

There are so many different types of chemical reactions and people have a variety of ways of classifying them. Rather than creating an exhaustive list, we'll focus on three main types of reactions as they help us learn a few key concepts.

Precipitation and Solubility

Have you ever stopped to wonder why salt dissolves in ocean water, but not shells and rocks? Chemical substances – both covalent and ionic – have different solubilities in water. As we saw in the solubility rules on the previous page, compounds containing sodium ions tend to soluble (so salt dissolves in water), but compounds containing carbonate (like the calcium carbonate of seashells) tend to be insoluble. While the solubility rules help us predict if something will be soluble in water or not, they do not explain *why* some compound dissolve and others do not.

The solubility of ionic compounds (we'll focus on other types of compounds at another time) depends on the strength of the bonds formed between the ions. Since the process of dissolving requires that water molecules break up and hydrate the ions, very strong bonds between ions prevent this from happening.

When two solutions containing ions are mixed, sometimes a ***precipitate*** is formed – an insoluble solid formed by two ions that make a very strong bond.

For example, we know that, according to the solubility rules, both potassium iodide (KI) and lead (II) nitrate ($Pb(NO_3)_2$) are soluble in water. when solutions of these two compounds are mixed, what happens?

3.1 In the instant that a solution of KI is mixed with a solution of $Pb(NO_3)_2$, what ions are present in the mixture?

3.2 Looking at the four ions you listed, what are the possible combinations of neutral compounds that *could* form?

3.3 Which of the compounds that you listed above are **insoluble** in water? _____

3.4 When aqueous solutions of ionic compounds are mixed, any ions that do not form insoluble solids remain in the aqueous state. Write a balanced reaction to show the reaction of KI (aq) with $Pb(NO_3)_2$ (aq). Indicate which product is in the solid phase (your insoluble solid from the previous question) and which ionic compound forms, but remains dissolved (aqueous).

The balanced equation you wrote in the question above is called the **conventional (or molecular) equation**. It is a balanced equation like we have seen already. It provides a bookkeeping of all the species present and arranged for neutral compounds.

Sometimes, especially with precipitation reactions like these, it can be helpful to keep track of all of our ions separately. In a **total ionic equation**, all the aqueous species are split up into their component ions. Much like you did in the first question in this part, all the ions are split up and written as aqueous. This helps us see which ions are present in solution and is a more accurate reflection of what the solution is really like: free-floating aqueous ions rather than neutral ionic compounds.

3.5 Again list the ions present when a solution of KI is mixed with a solution of $Pb(NO_3)_2$. On the product side of the arrow list the insoluble product as a neutral species in the solid state and any soluble compounds as separate aqueous ions. This is the **total ionic equation**.

The last type of reaction that we might find helpful shows us the reaction that is actually happening. Aqueous ions that remain in solution (that DON'T form an insoluble solid) are termed *spectator ions*. Spectator ions are spectators – they are not directly involved in any chemical or physical change in the reaction. In a **net ionic equation** we cancel any spectator ions that appear on both sides of the arrow, leaving only the species involved in our reaction.

3.6 Look at the total ionic equation that you wrote in the previous question. Rewrite the equation below, but cancel any aqueous ions that appear unchanged on both sides of the arrow. You should be left with only two ions reacting to form a solid precipitate. For example:

A^+ (aq) + ~~B^- (aq)~~ + ~~C^+ (aq)~~ + D^- (aq) → AD (s) + ~~B^- (aq)~~ + ~~C^+ (aq)~~   BECOMES A^+ (aq) + D^- (aq) → AD (s)

3.7 Predict the products and write the total ionic, net ionic, and conventional equations for the following reactions:

a) $Al(NO_3)_3$ (aq) + $Ba(OH)_2$ (aq) →

b) $CaCl_2$ (aq) + Na_2SO_4 (aq) →

Acid-Base Reactions

In the simplest type of acid-base reaction an acid and a base react to form an ionic compound and water. Let's define a few terms:

An **acid** is a compound that *donates* a proton (H^+). Common acids are HCl (stomach acid), citric acid (found in citrus fruits like lemons and oranges), acetic acid (vinegar), and ascorbic acid (Vitamin C).

A **base** is a compound that *accepts* a proton. Often we encounter bases with the formula MOH where M is a metal ion like Na^+ or K^+. The hydroxide ion (OH^-) is the part of the compound that acts a base, accepting a proton to form water.

3.8 Write a balanced equation to show a proton reacting with a hydroxide ion to form water.

The equation you wrote is the net ionic equation for *acid-base neutralization reactions.*

The generic complete equation for an acid-base neutralization reaction is:

$$HX\ (aq) + MOH\ (aq) \rightarrow MX\ (aq) + H_2O\ (l)$$

$$HX = acid,\ MOH = base,\ MX = ionic\ compound$$

3.9 Write the total ionic equation for the generic reaction given above.

Acids and bases can be grouped into the categories "strong" and "weak".

Strong acids fully dissociate in water, meaning that for every molecule of HX added to water you get an H^+ ion and an X^- ion – no HX molecules remain intact. You can think of a strong acid in the same way you think of a strong electrolyte – lots of ions are formed when dissolved in water. The strong acids you should be familiar with are: HCl, HBr, HI, nitric acid (HNO_3), sulfuric acid (H_2SO_4), perchloric acid ($HClO_4$) and chloric acid ($HClO_3$). *Note: H_2SO_4 has two protons it can donate, but only the first one fully dissociates: $H_2SO_4 \rightarrow H^+ + HSO_4^-$. HSO_4^- is a weak acid.*

Weak acids do not fully dissociate in water. When a weak acid is dissolved in water, only a few ions are formed (like a weak electrolyte). Most of the acid molecules remain intact. For example, HF is a weak acid. When dissolved in water only a few percent of the HF molecules break apart into H^+ and F^-. The rest remain neutral HF molecules. Weak acids you should know: HF, acetic acid (CH_3COOH), phosphoric acid (H_3PO_4), and any other acid you come across that isn't a strong acid.

3.10 Predict the products and write the total ionic, net ionic, and conventional equations for the following reactions:

    a) calcium hydroxide and hydroiodic acid

    b) lithium hydroxide and nitric acid

    c) barium hydroxide and sulfuric acid

We can combine what we know about acid-base reactions, stoichiometry, and concentration to predict how much acid or base we will need to neutralize a solution.

3.11 We need to neutralize 200.0 mL of a 0.1 M solution of $Ca(OH)_2$ before we can dispose of it safely. How many moles of hydroxide ion does this solution contain? *Remember that there are two hydroxide ions for every $Ca(OH)_2$ compound.*

3.12 We have a 2.0 M solution of HCl. How much of this solution do we need to add to our calcium hydroxide to neutralize all of the base?

3.13 Write a balanced equation to show the neutralization reaction and what the products of the reaction are.

Titration – An Application of Stoichiometry

A titration is using a solution of known concentration to find the concentration of an unknown solution. Typically, in general chemistry, this is done with an acid and a base, but titrations of other solutions are possible, too. The primary idea is that the known solution is added slowly (drop-wise) to the unknown solution until an *indicator* signals that the solution has been neutralized. An indicator is a substance that changes color when certain conditions happen. Let's look at an acid-base titration as an example.

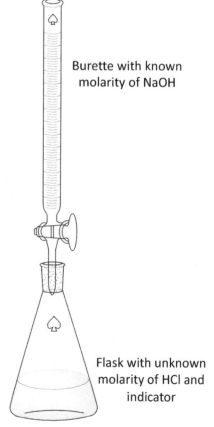

Burette with known molarity of NaOH

Let's say we have a solution of hydrochloric acid, but we don't know its concentration very accurately. We know it is somewhere between 0.5 - 0.9 M, but we need to know more exactly. In order to find the concentration, we place an accurately measured amount of the hydrochloric acid solution in to a flask. We use volumetric glassware to do this – glassware that is able to make very precise measurements. We will also use a sodium hydroxide solution that has a concentration we know very accurately as well. This solution goes in a burette with very accurate graduated markings. We use phenolphthalein as an indicator because it turns from clear to pink when we have neutralized our solution.

Flask with unknown molarity of HCl and indicator

The starting volume of NaOH is recorded and then the NaOH solution is added very slowly, drop by drop, until the indicator changes color and the solution is neutralized. At this point, the moles of HCl and the moles of NaOH added are equal to each other. The ending volume of the NaOH solution in the burette is recorded and the total volume of NaOH solution added is calculated.

3.14 Write a balanced equation for the acid-base neutralization reaction that occurs in this titration.

3.15 A 100.00 mL sample of our unknown HCl solution is added to a flask. A solution of NaOH with the concentration of 0.673 M is added to the burette. The titration is done and the indicator changes color after 123.18 mL of NaOH solution is added. How many moles of NaOH were added to the flask?

3.16 The number you calculated is the same number of moles of HCl in the flask. Since 100.00 mL of HCl solution was placed in the flask, what is the molarity of the HCl solution?

Oxidation-Reduction Reactions

The last type of reaction we will take a close look at is the oxidation reduction reaction, or "redox" reaction. In a redox reaction one or more electrons is transferred from one species to another. In order to tell if a redox reaction has happened, we need to be able to tell if a species gained or lost an electron. We do this by assigning oxidation numbers. an oxidation number is a bookkeeping way of keeping track of the oxidation state of an element or ion.

You have already learned how to assign the oxidation state of a single ion when you used the charges on ions to predict how many partners they need to make a neutral compound. For example:

- The oxidation state of an ion is equal to its charge. The oxidation state of Na^+, Li^+, K^+, etc. is +1.
- The oxidation state of Ca^{2+}, Mg^{2+}, Ba^{2+}, etc. is +2.
- The oxidation state Cl^-, Br^-, I^-, etc. is -1.

We can add a few more simple rules:

- The oxidation of a pure elemental substance is zero. For example, H_2, Na (not ionic), O_2, etc. all have a zero oxidation state.
- The oxidation state of hydrogen in a compound is +1.
- The oxidation state of oxygen in a compound is -2, unless it's hydrogen peroxide (H_2O_2), when it is -1.

With just one more rule, we can find the oxidation state of elements in nearly any compound:

- The oxidation states of each species must sum to the total charge of the compound (neutral = 0). For example, CH_4 is a neutral species. The oxidation state of *each* hydrogen is +1 (there are four of them), so the carbon must have an oxidation state of -4 to balance the charges to neutral.

3.17 Assign oxidation states to each of the elements in the following substances:

a) H_3PO_4 H: _____   P: _____   O: _____

b) H_2SO_4 H: _____   S: _____   O: _____

c) NH_4^+ H: _____   N: _____

d) NO_3^- O: _____   N: _____

Now that we know how to assign oxidation states we can use this skill to determine which oxidation states change in a redox reaction. Let's define a few terms:

Oxidized: A species is oxidized if it loses electrons in the reaction.

Reduced: A species is reduced if it gains electrons in a reaction.

It can be helpful to remember the mnemonic **OIL RIG** (Oxidation: I lose e⁻; Reduction: I gain e⁻)

3.18 Assign oxidation states to each element in the substances on both sides of the reaction.

$$2 \text{ Mg (s)} + O_2 \text{ (g)} \rightarrow 2 \text{ MgO}$$

Mg: ____ O: _____   →   Mg: _____ O: _____

Which species lost electrons in the reaction? _____

Which species gained electrons in the reaction? _____

Which species is oxidized in the reaction? _____

Which species is reduced in the reaction? _____

3.19 For each of the following reactions identify which species is reduced and which is oxidized.

a) Fe_2O_3 (s) + 2 Al (s) → 2Fe (s) + Al_2O_3 (s)

b) Mg (s) + 2 HCl (aq) → H_2 (g) + $MgCl_2$ (aq)

c) Cu (s) + 2 $AgNO_3$ (aq) → 2 Ag (s) + $Cu(NO_3)_2$ (aq)

3.20 Classify the reactions below as **precipitation, acid-base,** or **oxidation-reduction.**

a) H_2SO_4 (aq) + 2 H_2O (l) → SO_4^{2-} (aq) + 2 H_3O^+ (aq)

b) 2 Na (s) + 2 H_2O (l) → 2 NaOH (aq) + H_2 (g)

c) 3 $Ba(NO_3)_2$ (aq) + 2 K_3PO_4 (aq) → $Ba_3(PO_4)_2$ (s) + 6 KNO_3 (aq)

d) HF (aq) + KOH (aq) → H_2O (l) + KF (aq)

e) Na_2S (aq) + $Ca(NO_3)_2$ (aq) → CaS (s) + 2 $NaNO_3$ (aq)

f) Fe_2O_3 (s) + 2 Al (s) → Al_2O_3 (s) + 2 Fe (l)

Concept Map

Create a concept map using the following key words. You may add any additional words, as necessary.

Law of Conservation of Mass	balanced equation	mole ratios	stoichiometry	limiting reactant
solution	solute	solvent	soluble	insoluble
aqueous	molarity	dilution	strong electrolyte	weak electrolyte
nonelectrolyte	ionic compound	covalent compound	precipitate	spectator ion
acid	base	neutralization	titration	indicator
oxidation state	oxidation	reduction		

Unit 5

Gases

Part 1: The Behavior of Gases

Gas Pressure

Warm-Up Exercises

1.1. Write a brief description, in your own words, of how the air pressure in a room can be measured.

1.2. Convert 725 mm Hg to the following units:

   a) atm: _____   b) torr: _____   c) bar: _____

   d) kPa: _____   e) psi: _____

1.3. A sample of gas is placed in a manometer and mercury added. The atmospheric pressure is measured to be 752 mm Hg. What is the pressure of the gas sample?

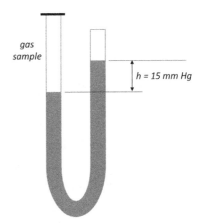

gas sample

h = 15 mm Hg

The Gas Laws

The gas laws describe and predict the behavior of gas samples as we change conditions like pressure, temperature, volume, and amount of gas. For the most part, these are intuitive relationships that you have experience with.

1.4 Describe what you think will happen to a sample of gas under the following conditions:

a) What will happen to the **pressure** of a sample of gas in a sealed tube if you squeeze (**compress**) the tube? (Circle your answer)

Pressure will increase   Pressure will decrease   No change

b) What will happen to the **volume** of a sample of gas in a flexible, sealed tube if you **heat** the tube? (Circle your answer)

Volume will increase   Volume will decrease   No change

c) What will happen to the **volume** of a sample of gas in a flexible tube if you **add more gas** to the tube? (Circle your answer)

Volume will increase   Volume will decrease   No change

1.5 Summarize these relationships here:

a) When volume decreases, pressure _____.

b) When temperature increases, volume _____.

c) When number of moles of a gas increases, volume _____.

These relationships describe the findings of Boyle, Charles, and Avogadro. In each of these relationships, all other factors must be held constant. For example, Boyle explored the relationship between volume and pressure while holding temperature and moles of gas constant. Charles explored the relationship between temperature and volume while holding moles and pressure constant. Avogadro studied the connection between volume and number of moles with pressure and temperature held constant. It is possible, however, to change more than one of these factors at a time if we know how they are all related to each other.

When two things are linearly related to each other, we can say they are proportional. For example, volume is proportional to temperature:

$$V \alpha T$$

When two things are proportional, we can write them as related to each other through a constant:

$$V = c \times T, \text{ where c is a constant}$$

In our summary of volume, pressure, temperature and moles relationships, we find the following

$$V \alpha \frac{nT}{P}$$

1.6 Rewrite the proportionality above using a constant and an equals sign. Assign the letter R as your constant.

1.7 Rewrite your equation, above, so that pressure times volume is on the left side of the equation.

This is the **Ideal Gas Law**. It describes the behavior of gases under a variety of conditions and allows us to predict the result of changes in pressure, temperature, volume, and moles of gas.

R, the constant you used, is the **Ideal Gas Constant** and has two different values depending on the constants you are using.

$$R = 0.082057 \frac{L \cdot atm}{mol \cdot K} \quad \text{or} \quad R = 8.3145 \frac{J}{mol \cdot K}$$

1.8 In a problem where we are working with a gas sample measured in liters, with gas pressure in atmospheres, and the temperature in Kelvin, which value of R should we use?

1.9 What is the pressure exerted by 1.00×10^{20} molecules of N_2 gas in a 305 mL flask at 175 °C?

The Ideal Gas Law allows us change a lot of variables at one, but sometimes we're only changing one variable (like pressure) and we want to see how something else (like volume) will change. If we are holding all the other parts of our sample constant (n, R, and T in this case), we can set up a relationship like this:

$$P_1V_1 = nRT = P_2V_2 \text{ or simply } P_1V_1 = P_2V_2$$

1.10 Create a similar expression showing the relationship between volume and temperature when we hold n and pressure constant.

1.11 If a 2.0 L balloon is taken from sea level (1.0 atm of pressure) to Denver, Colorado (0.76 atm of pressure), what would its new volume be? (Assume temperature stays constant).

1.12 I have the same 2.0 L balloon at 298 K (the temperature of a warm room). What temperature would I have to heat or cool it to for it to be the same volume as in the question above?

Gas Density and Partial Pressure

Since we now have a way to relate the various conditions our gas sample is under, let's see some other uses for the Ideal Gas Law.

1.13 The density of a substance is calculated using mass/volume. If we have a certain number of moles of a sample of gas, how can we determine what mass we have?

1.14 Rearrange the Ideal Gas Law (PV = nRT) to solve for the density of a gas (d) in terms of pressure, molar mass, and temperature.

Using the equation for gas density can also help us determine the molecular weight of an unknown substance. Imagine a scenario where we vaporize an unknown solid of a particular mass in a sealed chamber of known volume.

1.15 Rearrange your equation for gas density to solve for molar mass in terms of density, pressure, and temperature.

1.16 A 0.76 g sample of an unknown solid was vaporized in a 345-mL vessel. If the vapor has a pressure of 985 mmHg at 148 °C, what is the molecular weight of the solid?

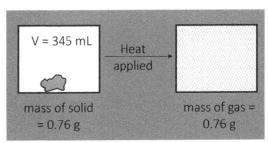

One more aspect of gas samples we should examine is samples that are mixtures of gases. As you probably know, the air we breathe is a mixture of nitrogen and oxygen, with trace amounts of other gases like carbon dioxide, neon, argon, etc. How can we handle these mixtures in terms of pressure and gas density?

Dalton's Law of Partial Pressures helps us out here. Dalton determined that the total pressure of a gas sample is simply the sum of the individual pressures of each gas in the mixture. For example, if I mix a sample of gas A that is 200 torr with a sample of gas B that is 500 torr, the resulting mixture will have a total pressure of 700 torr (provided we have held temperature and volume constant).

It's fairly straightforward to see how this works mathematically. If we think about a mixture of gases in terms of moles, we can rearrange the Ideal Gas Law to help us sum those moles and determine total pressure.

A mixture of gases can be defined as the sum of moles of each gas: $n_{total} = n_1 + n_2 + n_3 + \dots$

The Ideal Gas Law can be rearranged to solve for n: $\qquad n = \dfrac{PV}{RT}$

Combing these two equations: $\quad n_{total} = \dfrac{P_{total}V}{RT} = \dfrac{P_1V}{RT} + \dfrac{P_2V}{RT} + \dfrac{P_3V}{RT} + \dots$

Here, we can see that, if V and T are held constant, $P_{total} = P_1 + P_2 + P_3 + \dots$

Let's introduce the definition of **mole fraction (χ)**: the ratio of the number of moles of a component in a mixture to the total number of moles in the mixture.

$$\chi_1 = \frac{n_1}{n_{total}} = \frac{n_1}{n_1 + n_2 + n_3 + \dots}$$

If we use mole fraction, we can restate the pressure of each component as a pressure related to the mole fraction.

1.17 We have a mixture of three gases with a total pressure equal to P_{total}. Express the pressure of each separate gas (P_1, P_2, P_3) in terms of the mole fraction (χ_1, χ_2, χ_3) and total pressure.

1.18 The air we breathe is a mixture of 80% nitrogen and 20% oxygen. If the total pressure is 1.0 atm, what is the partial pressure of nitrogen and oxygen that you breathe?

1.19 Our bodies require the partial pressure of oxygen to be near 0.21 atm in the air we breathe. If a SCUBA diver is breathing air under 30 m of water, the air mix is under about 4.0 atm total pressure. What percentage of oxygen should the tank hold to deliver the correct partial pressure of oxygen to the diver?

Part 2: Kinetic Molecular Theory

While the gas laws do a good job of explaining gas behavior (under ideal conditions), they do not make any effort to explain *why* we observe these behaviors. That is where **Kinetic Molecular Theory** comes in. Kinetic Molecular Theory is a set of ideas that provides a theoretical explanation of gas behavior at the particulate level. Remember, *laws* describe macroscopic, observed behavior; *theories* explain that behavior and are subject to change as we make more observations through experiments.

Here are the main points of Kinetic Molecular Theory:

- Gas particles are so small compared to the container they are held in that their volumes are negligible. This means that, for example, if you have a balloon full of air the molecules of gas essentially take up no space in the balloon.
- Gas particles are in constant, random motion.
- Gas particles are constantly colliding with each other and with the container walls. The collision of the particles with the walls are the cause of the pressure exerted by the gas.
- When the particles collide, the collisions are *elastic* – no energy is lost through the collisions.
- The particles do not interact with each other – they do not attract or repel each other.

We can sum these up with the main idea:

Gases are a collection of non-interacting point particles.

Furthermore:

Pressure arises from molecules colliding with container walls.

Temperature is directly related to the kinetic energy of the gas molecules. The more kinetic energy the particles have, the greater their temperature.

Gas Velocity

How fast are gas particles traveling when they collide into the container walls? The velocity of gas particles is a range – there are many slow moving particles and many fast moving particles. We can, though, derive a way to determine the **root mean square velocity** of a gas sample. RMS velocity is the speed of a molecule that has the average kinetic energy for the sample. While the derivation itself is not critical to understanding the idea of RMS velocity, it can help to understand the process. Essentially, if we take the total kinetic energy of 1 mol of gas and divide it evenly among all the molecules in that mole we can determine the velocity of a molecule with the average velocity based on the kinetic energy of the sample. There are two factors that influence this velocity.

2.1 What measurement do we use to determine the kinetic energy of a sample of gas? (*Hint: See above*).

2.2 A moving object has kinetic energy equal to $\frac{1}{2}mv^2$. If we are solving for the velocity of a gas particle, what else must we know about it?

The RMS velocity of a gas molecule (or atom) can be found using the following equation:

$$u_{rms} = \sqrt{\frac{3RT}{M}}$$

Where u_{rms} = the root mean square velocity of the particle; R = the gas constant, T = temperature, M = molar mass

Let's do a quick unit analysis to determine the correct units for our equation.

2.3 The derivation of the equation, above comes from the following equality:

$$\frac{1}{2}mv^2 = \frac{1}{N_A}\left(\frac{3}{2}RT\right)$$

In this equality, SI units of kg (for mass), m, s (for velocity, in m/s), and Kelvin (for T) are used. The N_A is Avogadro's number.

Which units of R are appropriate in this formula? (Remember, 1 J = 1 $\frac{kg \cdot m^2}{s^2}$)

$$R = 0.082057\ \frac{L \cdot atm}{mol \cdot K} \quad \text{or} \quad R = 8.3145\ \frac{J}{mol \cdot K}$$

2.4 The large M in the RMS velocity equation is molar mass, but comes from $m \cdot N_A$. Should molar mass, in this case, be expressed in grams/mol or kilograms/mol?

2.5 What is the u_{rms} for N_2 at 298 K? (Remember that molar mass for nitrogen gas MUST be in kg/mol.)

2.6 If the gas sample in the previous question is heated up, what happens to the RMS velocity? (Circle your answer).

    RMS velocity will increase   RMS velocity will decrease   No change

2.7 If the gas in the previous question is changed from nitrogen to chlorine gas, what happens to the RMS velocity? (Circle your answer)

    RMS velocity will increase   RMS velocity will decrease   No change

Diffusion and Effusion

If gas particles are moving so quickly, why does it take so long to smell someone perfume when they walk into a room? It's important to remember that gas particles travel in a straight line *until they collide with another particle.* They do not have an uninterrupted path across the room.

The process of gases mixing is called diffusion. If two gases are allowed to mix, diffusion will eventually lead to a homogeneous mixture with the gas particles uniformly distributed throughout the container.

The rate of diffusion is proportional to the RMS velocity of the sample, so lighter particles will have a higher rate of diffusion, and heavier particles will diffuse more slowly.

Effusion is a special case of diffusion in which a mixture of gases is released into an evacuated container. The lighter particles move into the container more quickly than the heavier ones. A repeated process of effusion – release of a gas mixture into an empty, quick closure of the gas source, release of the new gas mixture into an empty container, and so on – can be used to separate a mixture of gases. A similar process was used to enrich uranium (by separating U-235 from U-238) in the making of the first atomic bomb.

2.8 A sample of helium gas and a sample of argon gas are both released across the room from you. Which gas will reach you first?

2.9 Ammonia gas (NH_3) and hydrogen chloride gas (HCl) react when they meet to form a white powder (NH_4Cl). If the two gases are released at the same time from opposite ends of a sealed glass tube, where will the powder form? (Circle your answer)

NH₃ gas   HCl gas

Closer to the NH_3 end   In the middle   Closer to the HCl end

Real Gases

Our last brief topic addresses when ideal gases are not ideal. Generally speaking, there is no such thing as an "ideal gas". There are conditions, however, under which a gas will behave ideally.

Remember that the main points of kinetic molecular theory are that 1) particle size is negligible and 2) particles don't interact.

2.10 What are some conditions under which the size of gas particles might become non-negligible? Consider factors like pressure, temperature, volume, etc.

2.11 What are some conditions under which gas particles might be forced close enough to each other that they might start to interact? Consider factors like pressure, temperature, volume, etc.

As we raise the pressure of a system (by compressing the volume, for example), gas particles are forced closer to each other and their actual physical volume can start to take up space in the container. At very high pressure, the effective volume we observe ($V_{effective}$) is different from the ideal volume (V_{ideal}) because of the volume of the gas particles themselves.

Similarly, at high pressures or very low temperatures, gas particles may get close enough to each other to start to interact. When this happens their collisions are no longer elastic and the observed pressure (P_{obs}) differs from the ideal pressure (P_{ideal}) because of a reduction in the pressure exerted by the particles.

Van der Waal was able to derive a formula that allows us to correct the ideal gas law for gases that are not behaving ideally – these are called "real gases".

$$\left[P_{obs} + a\left(\frac{n}{V}\right)^2 \right][V - nb] = nRT$$

a and b are experimentally-determined constants that vary by gas

- a depends on the forces the particles exert on each other.
- b increases with the size of the molecule.

Values for a and b are called "Van der Waals constants" and can be looked up in tables by substance.

2.12 Which gas would you expect to have a higher value for b: helium or argon? Why?

2.13 Polar molecules tend to exert greater forces on each other than non-polar molecules. Which gas would you expect to have a higher value for a: oxygen or water? Why?

Concept Map

Create a concept map using the following key words. You may add any additional words, as necessary.

pressure	temperature	kinetic energy	volume	moles of gas
density	molar mass	RMS velocity	mole fraction	partial pressure
elastic collision	ideal gas	real gas	diffusion	effusion

Unit 6

Thermochemistry

Part 1: Energy, Heat, and Work

Energy

Warm-Up Exercises

1.1. Energy can be divided into two main categories. Give a brief description of each type and some examples of each. Be sure to include at least one example for each that is directly related to chemistry.

1.2. The Law of Conservation of Energy says that energy is neither created nor destroyed. Give a few examples of energy being converted from potential to kinetic or *vice versa*.

1.3. In chemistry, especially when we are studying thermodynamics, it is important to keep track of what makes up the *system* and what makes up the *surroundings*. In the following examples, determine what the system is and what the surrounding are. What direction is heat flowing: from system to surroundings or from surroundings to system?

    a) A log burning in a fire

    b) An ice cube melting on a countertop

    c) A hot pan sitting on the stove (which is off)

1.4. Convert the following values to the new set of units:

a) 10.0 cal = _____ J

b) 120.0 kcal = _____ kWh

c) 418 J = _____ cal

Energy Flow

As we learned while studying chemical bonds, bonds form between atoms in a way that minimizes the total energy of the system. In order to break a chemical bond, we must put energy into the system. Energy diagrams are a graphical way of showing the energy flow during a process such as bond-making or bond-breaking (or in the case of a chemical reaction, both!).

1.5 Sketch an energy diagram to show two individual hydrogen atoms coming together to form hydrogen gas. Is the hydrogen molecule higher or lower in energy than the individual atoms?

1.6 For the reaction above, what direction does energy flow due to the change in energy between the individual hydrogen atoms and the hydrogen molecule? What is the sign of E_{system} in this case?

1.7 Sketch an energy diagram to represent the reverse process: breaking the H-H bond to form two individual hydrogen atoms. What direction would energy flow in this reaction? What is the sign of E_{system} in this case?

Heat and Work

Energy is exchanged between the system and the surroundings through *heat* and *work*. Heat (designated as q) is thermal energy. Work (designated as w) is work energy. We'll look more closely at heat before we turn our attention to work. We can quantify the energy change in a system as ΔE.

$$\Delta E = q + w$$

It is important to keep track of the proper use of signs for changes in heat and work.

1.8 Complete the following table:

Sign conventions for q, w, and ΔE

q (heat)	___ system gains thermal energy	___ system loses thermal energy
w (work)	___ work done on the system	___ work done by the system
ΔE (change in internal energy of the system)	___ energy flows into the system	___ energy flows out of the system

State Functions

A state function is a property of a system that depends only on its state at a given instant and not on how the system reached that state. Internal energy of a system is a state function. Heat and work are not. Practically, what this means, is that some systems are capable of doing a large an=mount of work, while losing very little energy to heat. Other systems, however, can do very little work since much of their internal energy is lost to heat. For example, an internal combustion engine is fueled by gasoline (which stores a lot of energy). The work done by the engine is used to move the car, but a significant amount of the energy from the fuel is lot to the surroundings as heat and is not available to do the work to move the car. An electric car, on the other hand, stores energy in batteries. The amount of heat generated is much smaller so the amount of useful work from the batteries is a much higher portion of the total energy.

Exothermic vs. Endothermic Processes

A process is defined as *exothermic* if heat is transferred to the surroundings (q < 0, heat is lost).

A process is defined as *endothermic* is heat is transferred to the system (q > 0, heat is gained).

It is critical to clearly define the system and the surroundings for these processes. We can measure heat using a change in temperature, but it is important to remember that we usually measure the temperature of the surroundings. When heat is lost by the system, it flows to the surroundings and we can measure that increase in heat of the surroundings as a rise in temperature.

1.9 Classify the following processes as exothermic or endothermic.

    a) A log burning in a fire

    b) An ice cube melting on a countertop

    c) A hot pan sitting on the stove (which is off)

Heat Capacity

Temperature is not heat, it is how we measure it. Experiments show that heat is proportional to temperature, but some substances are capable of absorbing more heat (q) than others with the same increase in temperature. For example, water can absorb a significant amount of heat before the temperature rises appreciably. A rock, however, will show a much greater increase in temperature if the same amount of heat is transferred to it. The difference between these two substances is their *heat capacity*. The heat capacity (C) of a system is the amount of heat required to change its temperature by 1 °C.

$$C = \frac{q}{\Delta T} \ (units \ are \ \frac{J}{°C})$$

The heat capacity of a system depends on a) how much of a substance you are heating and b) the **specific heat capacity** of that substance (*the amount of heat required to raise 1 gram of the substance by 1 °C*).

The heat capacity of a system is an **extensive property** – it depends on how much you have. The more water you have, the more heat is required to raise the temperature.

The _specific_ heat capacity of a substance is an **intensive property** – it only depends on the type of substance, not the amount. he amount of heat required to raise the temperature of 1 gram of water is different from that needed to raise the temperature of 1 gram of rock.

We can use the specific heat capacity of a substance to predict the increase in temperature we can expect to see when a certain amount of heat is added to it. The formula is similar to that for the heat capacity of a system, but we must take mass into consideration.

$$q = m \times C_s \times \Delta T$$

Here m = mass (in grams), C_s is the specific heat of the substance, and temperature is measured in Celsius.

The specific heat capacities of some common substances are listed here:

Substance	Specific Heat Capacity (J/g·°C)
Gold	0.128
Copper	0.385
Aluminum	0.903
Water	4.18
Ethanol	2.42
Glass	0.750
Granite	0.790
Sand	0.840

1.10 Which substance would require the most heat to raise it 1 °C? Which substance would require the least amount of heat to raise it 1 °C?

1.11 Let's say you have samples of three different substances all at 25.0 °C: 100.0 grams of water, 100.0 grams of granite, and 100.0 of aluminum. Each sample is heated with 500.0 J of energy (q = 500.0 J). What is the resulting temperature of each substance?

Thermal Energy Transfer

When two objects of different temperatures are placed in contact with each other, heat flows from the hotter object to the cooler object until both objects reach thermal equilibrium – their temperatures are the same and no additional heat flows in either direction. We can use the Law of Conservation of Energy to predict that the heat lost by one object must be exactly equal to the heat gained by the other. Using our equation relating heat to specific heat capacity, we are able to predict what the final temperature of each substance is, provided we have enough information about each substance.

We know that the heat of the hotter substance A must flow completely to the cooler substance B, so q_A = -q_B. Using our equation from earlier, we can relate the two values in this way:

$$q_A = m_A \times C_{s(A)} \times \Delta T_A = -q_B = -m_B \times C_{s(B)} \times \Delta T_B$$

In order to solve a problem like this we need to know masses of each substance along with their specific heat capacities. We also need some information about starting temperatures and to remember that the final temperature of *both substances* will be the same.

1.12 A 15.0 gram aluminum ball at 25.0 °C is placed into 150.0 grams of hot water (47.0 °C). What is the final temperature of the system at thermal equilibrium?

Now that we have discussed heat exchange in systems, it's time to turn our attention to when systems do work on their surroundings. Let's use a fairly simple example. Suppose an amount of heat is applied to a hot air balloon. As we know from the gas laws, when the temperature is increased, the gas will expand. The expansion of the gas in the hot air balloon pushes on the atmosphere – it does work on the atmosphere. This is called pressure-volume work. Let's explore some of the energy changes in this system.

Pressure-Volume Work

Pressure-volume (PV) work is the expansion of gas against a constant external pressure. We can calculate the work done based on the external pressure and the change in volume.

$$w = -P_{external}\Delta V$$

$P_{external}$ is the external pressure and ΔV is the total change in volume of the system.

1.13 A hot air balloon at 1atm is heated with 1.3×10^8 J of heat causing the volume to increase from 4×10^6 L to 4.5×10^6 L. How much energy does the gas lose as work in this process and what is the energy change (ΔE) of the gas. Let's break this into two parts:

a) How much work is done by heating the gas? What is the sign of your answer (+ or -)? What does the sign indicate?

b) Note that your answer to part a) is in the units of L·atm. In order to convert this answer to Joules, it is helpful to know one more version of R (the gas constant).

$$R = 8.314 \ \frac{J}{mol \cdot K} = 0.08206 \ \frac{L \cdot atm}{mol \cdot K} = 101.3 \ \frac{J}{L \cdot atm}$$

What is your answer to part a) in J? What is the sign of your answer (+ or -)? What does the sign indicate?

c) What is ΔE for this process? Remember: $\Delta E = q + w$.

d) Has the overall energy of the system increased or decreased?

Part 2: Enthalpy

Constant-Volume Calorimetry

Now we have a way of measuring the energy change of a system: we can measure q and w to find ΔE. Usually this is easier to do when volume is constant (instead of changing as in our last example). In a case where there is no change in volume, w = 0 and $\Delta E_{system} = q_{system}$.

Let's say you want to know how much energy is stored in a particular molecule. Since you cannot find the temperature change of each individual molecule in a reaction, it is easiest to measure the change in the temperature of the surroundings. If we can isolate the surroundings from other sources of heat (by insulating them, for example), we can measure the change in temperature that comes from the reaction alone. This is how calorimetry is done and is used to measure the energetics of all types of chemical reactions – including how much energy is stored in food.

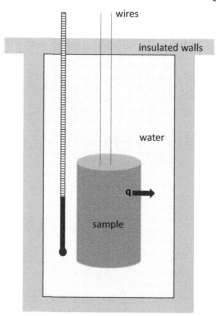

The figure to the right shows a "bomb calorimeter" in which a substance is burned in the presence of oxygen inside a sample chamber with no change in volume. All of the energy change from the burning of the sample is released as heat and transferred to the surrounding water. We measure the temperature change of the water to calculate the value of q.

We need to know the heat capacity of the entire calorimeter (C_{cal}) before we can gain any usable information. This is usually determined by burning a standard substance that gives of a known amount of heat. Then we can find the heat given off by the reaction via the following equations:

$$q_{cal} = C_{cal} \times \Delta T = -q_{rxn}$$

Since this reaction occurs with no change in volume, $\Delta E_{rxn} = q_{rxn}$. (*Note:* When a process is done at constant volume $q_{rxn} = q_v$)

2.1 In order to determine the number of kcal (food calories) in a teaspoon of sugar, we can do the following experiment in a bomb calorimeter. A 4.2 g sample of sucrose (1 teaspoon of sugar) is placed into a bomb calorimeter and burned in the presence of oxygen gas. The heat capacity of the calorimeter is 4.90 kJ/°C. The temperature of the water in the calorimeter rises from 23.6 °C to 37.8 °C.

a) What is the value of q_v in kJ?

b) What is this value in kcal (food calories)? (1 cal = 4.1855 J)

Chemical Reactions and Enthalpy

Using a bomb calorimeter to determine the change in energy due to chemical reactions is not always a very practical way to explore these processes. Most chemical reactions happen at constant pressure, not constant volume. When you burn a log in a fire or do a reaction in a beaker, the system is at constant atmospheric pressure and energy can be in the form of heat *and* work. Often we are only concerned with the heat produced (or required), not the work done. If you turn on your stove to boil water for pasta you are not concerned with how much work is done on the surroundings by the expansion of air...just how much heat is going into the pot of water (i.e., how long will it take to boil?).

We can now introduce the thermodynamic quantity *enthalpy (H)*: the amount of heat given off by a process under constant pressure. The enthalpy of a system is the sum of its internal energy and the product of its pressure and volume.

$$H = E + PV$$

We are usually more concerned with the change in enthalpy for a process:

$$\Delta H = \Delta E + P\Delta V$$

Since $P\Delta V$ represents the work done by a system (-w) and ΔE is the sum of heat (q_p, when at constant pressure) and work, then we can determine that the enthalpy change of a system is equal to the heat at constant pressure:

$$\Delta H = q_p$$

For the most part, ΔH is close to ΔE (for systems that do not do much work on the surroundings). Exceptions to this are systems that produce or consume large amounts of gas. We will study these more closely when we revisit thermodynamics in terms of entropy changes.

We now have an additional way to define exothermic and endothermic processes:

A process is defined as *exothermic* if heat is transferred to the surroundings (q < 0, heat is lost to the surroundings, **ΔH is negative**).

A process is defined as *endothermic* is heat is transferred to the system (q > 0, heat is absorbed from the surroundings, **ΔH is positive**).

2.2 Identify the following processes as exothermic or endothermic and give the sign of ΔH for each.

   a) An ice cube melting on the countertop

   b) Sweat evaporating from skin

   c) A log burning in the fire

Enthalpy of Chemical Reactions

When a reaction happens, where does the enthalpy come from? Molecules are one of the most compact ways to store energy. We use energy stored in chemical bonds all the time: energy is stored in food, in gasoline, and in the methane we use to heat our homes. When an exothermic chemical reaction happens we reorganize the chemical bonds in a way that make them more stable, releasing the extra stored energy as heat. Endothermic reactions are the opposite, we put heat energy in and that energy is stored in less stable chemical bonds that we can use later.

Energy is **required** to *break bonds*. Energy is **released** when we *make bonds*.

Not all chemical bonds are the same: some are weaker than others, some are stronger than others. The strength of the bond is related to the energy stored there.

Every chemical reaction has an associated enthalpy change (ΔH) called the **enthalpy of reaction**. This value depends on the amount of substance involved in the reaction as is always reported based on the balanced chemical equation with the smallest integer values and is reported in kJ.

For example, in the chemical reaction:

$$A + 2\,B \rightarrow AB_2 \qquad\qquad \Delta H_{rxn} = -50.0 \text{ kJ}$$

This represents the heat emitted when 1 mol of A reacts with 2 mol of B. If we have more or less of these quantities, we must scale the enthalpy accordingly.

2.3 Using the balanced reaction, above, how much heat is emitted from the reaction with 4 moles of A?

2.4 Using natural gas to heat your home has the following reaction and enthalpy:

$$CH_4\,(g) + 2\,O_2\,(g) \rightarrow CO_2\,(g) + 2\,H_2O\,(g) \qquad\qquad \Delta H_{rxn} = -802.3 \text{ kJ}$$

How many kJ of heat are produced by burning 250.0 g of methane (CH_4)?

We can directly measure the enthalpy of a chemical process if we conduct that process at constant pressure (rather than at constant volume). An example of this is a coffee-cup calorimeter: an insulated cup fitted with a thermometer. The chemical process (usually conducted in water) creates a change in temperature that can be measured. The value of q_{soln} can be found using:

$$q_{soln} = C_{soln} \times m_{soln} \times \Delta T = -q_{rxn}$$

We can find ΔH_{rxn} by dividing q_{rxn} by the number of moles reacted:

$$\Delta H_{rxn} = \frac{q_{rxn}}{n}$$

2.5 Let's say we place 25.0 mL of 1.0 M aqueous HCl in a coffee-cup calorimeter and measure the temperature to be 18.5 °C. We quickly add 25.0 mL of 1.0 M NaOH solution and this causes the temperature to rise to 25.0 °C. What is ΔH_{rxn} for the reaction? Assume that the density of the solution is that of water (1.00 g/mL) and that C_{soln} = 4.46 J/g·°C).

Hess's Law

As we just learned, since we must scale ΔH_{rxn} based on the amount of a substance we have, enthalpy must be an extensive quantity. There are a few tricks we can learn to use so that we can solve some trickier problems without resorting to calorimetry all the time.

1. If a chemical equation is multiplied by some factor, the ΔH_{rxn} is also multiplied by that factor.

2. If a chemical equation is reversed, the sign of ΔH_{rxn} is changed.

3. If a chemical reaction can be expressed as the sum of a series of steps, then ΔH_{rxn} for the overall reaction is the sum of the enthalpies for each step. This is known as **Hess's Law**.

2.6 What is the enthalpy change associated with changing graphite into diamond? Note: This would be a very difficult reaction, indeed, to carry out in a coffee-cup calorimeter. The following enthalpy values are known:

$$C \text{ (s, graphite)} + O_2 \text{ (g)} \rightarrow CO_2 \text{ (g)} \qquad \Delta H_{rxn} = -394 \text{ kJ}$$

$$C \text{ (s, diamond)} + O_2 \text{ (g)} \rightarrow CO_2 \text{ (g)} \qquad \Delta H_{rxn} = -396 \text{ kJ}$$

a) What is the value of ΔH_{rxn} overall for the conversion of graphite to diamond?

b) Is this an exothermic or endothermic process?

c) What is the ΔH_{rxn} for the reverse process (converting diamond to graphite)? Is it exothermic or endothermic?

Enthalpy of Formation

In the example above it was helpful to use the combustion data for carbon to find the enthalpy value we were looking for. It turns out we have a much more comprehensive list of *standardized* enthalpy values in the Table of Standard Enthalpies of Formation. Before we can use these we need to define what it means to be standardized.

Many thermodynamic values and functions depend on the concentration (or pressure) and temperature of the substances involved. Since we can't measure absolute values for enthalpies (only changes in enthalpy), we need a common reference point for these values. Chemistry uses **standard state** as this reference point and defines it in this way:

> compounds: pure substance in its normal phase at pressure = 1 atm

> solutions: a concentration of 1 M

> elements: the most stable form of an element at pressure = 1 atm

Thermodynamic data is usually reported a 25 °C, but there is *no specified standard temperature* for thermodynamic values. As a result, we must always give the state of the substance (solid, liquid, gas, aqueous) in our equations.

Standard state is indicated with the symbol: ° (as in ΔH°_{rxn}).

2.7 What is the standard state of the following substances under the following conditions?

> a) H_2 at 25 °C and 1 atm   b) Ag at 25 °C and 1 atm   c) H_2O at 125 °C and 1 atm

_____   _____   _____

The **Standard Enthalpy of Formation** (ΔH°_f) is the enthalpy change associated with the formation of one mole of a substance from its elements (all in their standard states) at 25 °C. A table of these values can be found in the appendix of any chemistry textbook.

Some examples:

> H_2 (g) + ½ O_2 (g) → H_2O (l) ΔH°_f = -285.8 kJ/mol

> Mg (s) + ½ O_2 (g) → MgO (s) ΔH°_f = -601.6 kJ/mol

> C (s, graphite) → C (s, diamond) ΔH°_f = 1.88 kJ/mol

Note: By definition, ΔH°_f = 0 for elements in their standard states at 25 °C .

Now we can write a generalized expression for Hess's Law that we can use for *any* reaction if we have heats of formation available:

$$\Delta H_{rxn} = \sum_n n \cdot \Delta H^\circ_{f,products} - \sum_m m \cdot \Delta H^\circ_{f,reactants}$$

In this equation, *n* and *m* represent the stoichiometric coefficients of the products and reactants. Putting this equation into words: The enthalpy of reaction is the sum of the heats of formation of the products (multiplied by their coefficients) minus the sum of the heats of formation of the reactants (multiplied by their coefficients). Essentially we are taking apart all of the reactants into their standard state elements and then reassembling these elements into the products. Since ΔH is a state function (doesn't depend on the path we take to get there), this is a valid approach!

2.8 Calculate ΔH for the following reaction:

$H_2(g) + Cl_2(g) \rightarrow 2HCl(g)$

Given the following:

$NH_3(g) + HCl(g) \rightarrow NH_4Cl(s)$	$\Delta H = -176$ kJ
$N_2(g) + 3 H_2(g) \rightarrow 2 NH_3(g)$	$\Delta H = -92$ kJ
$N_2(g) + 4 H_2(g) + Cl_2(g) \rightarrow 2 NH_4Cl(s)$	$\Delta H = -629$ kJ

2.9 Use the following heats of formation to determine $\Delta H°_{rxn}$ for the following process:

$3 KBr(s) + H_3PO_4(aq) \rightarrow K_3PO_4(aq) + 3 HBr(g)$

Substance	$\Delta H°_f$ (kJ/mol)	Substance	$\Delta H°_f$ (kJ/mol)
KBr (s)	394.1	K_3PO_4 (aq)	-2036
H_3PO_4 (aq)	-1280.	HBr (g)	-121.6

Concept Map

Create a concept map using the following key words. You may add any additional words, as necessary.

kinetic energy	potential energy	system	surroundings	internal energy
heat	work	state function	process function	exothermic
endothermic	heat capacity	extensive property	intensive property	thermal energy transfer
PV work	calorimetry	energy	enthalpy	standard state
heat of formation				

Unit 7

Liquids and Solutions

Part 1: Intermolecular Forces

Solids, Liquids and Gases

Warm-Up Exercises

1.1. In the boxes below, sketch pictures for how the molecules or atoms are distributed in a solid, liquid, and gas.

Solid	Liquid	Gas

1.2. List a few properties of each state of matter.

Solid:

Liquid:

Gas:

Intermolecular Forces

We know turn our attention to the bulk properties of matter – rather than focus on the individual particles, how do these particles interact with each other to forms solids, liquids, and gases? Understanding intermolecular forces helps us understand why some liquids have very high boiling points while others have low boiling points; why some liquids are very viscous while others are thin and more fluid; why some liquids mix together while others separate; why some solids will dissolve in one liquid, but not another. Let's start by defining the various types of **intermolecular forces**: the forces that act between molecules, ions and atoms and hold them together.

Dispersion Forces (London or Van der Waal's Force)

> The simplest type of force is experienced by all molecules, but is the dominant force in non-polar molecules. When two non-polar molecules get near each other their electrons can start to interact and repel each other. This creates a slight polarity in the two molecules as some electrons move toward one side of the molecule. The interaction is weak and short-lived, but can be significant for large molecules.

1.3 Sketch a diagram of two non-polar molecules inducing a momentary polarity as they approach each other. You may want to draw this in two or three steps (before and after, or before, during, after).

1.4 List some molecules that you would expect to experience only London Dispersion Forces in the liquid state. What is the main feature of the molecules that you used to decide?

Dipole-Dipole Forces

When polar molecules are in the liquid state, their poles align to minimize electron-electron repulsion and maximize the attraction between opposite poles (like charges repel, opposites attract). This attraction between poles holds the molecules together more strongly than London dispersion forces, so polar molecules of similar mass / size as non-polar molecules are held together more tightly.

1.5 Sketch a diagram of three or four polar molecules interacting through dipole-dipole forces. Be sure to show which end of each molecule has a slight positive charge and which end is negative.

1.6 List some molecules that you would expect to experience dipole-dipole forces as their dominant intermolecular force.

Hydrogen Bonding

Hydrogen bonding is a special case of dipole-dipole forces. In molecules that contain an O-H, N-H, or F-H bond, dipole-dipole forces are extremely strong. These particular bonds are very polar (remember electronegativity?) and the hydrogen atom is very small so the molecules can get very close to each other. In a hydrogen bond, the hydrogen atom forms a slight bond with the lone pair on the O, N, or F from another molecule nearby.

1.7 Sketch a diagram of three molecules of methanol (CH_3OH) interacting through hydrogen bonds. Show the hydrogen bond using a dashed line.

1.8 List some molecules that you would expect to experience hydrogen bonds as their dominant intermolecular force.

Those are the three main types of intermolecular forces for pure substances. Other forces and interactions are possible. For example, when ions are dissolved in a solution with polar molecules *ion-dipole forces* can result.

Intermolecular forces are especially important to understanding the behavior of liquids. They influence boiling points especially since boiling requires molecules escape the liquid phase, breaking the intermolecular forces that hold them together.

1.9 In the following pairs of molecules, predict which molecule will have the higher boiling point. Why did you choose that one?

a) CH_3Cl or CH_3OH

b) CH_3CH_2OH or $HOCH_2CH_2OH$

c) $CH_3CH_2CH_2CH_2CH_3$ (pentane) or $C(CH_3)_4$ (neopentane)

Implications of Intermolecular Forces

There are three main properties that we can observe in liquids that are also the direct result of intermolecular forces (in addition to other properties that we will study further such as boiling point, vapor pressure, etc.)

Surface Tension: A liquid's resistance to an increase in surface area.

You may have noticed that many liquids tend to "bead up" on a surface. If a liquid were to spread out smoothly on a surface it would greatly increase the surface area of that liquid. Liquids with strong intermolecular forces tend to resist this increase in surface area and hold molecules closely together to form sphere-like shapes (decreasing the overall surface area).

Capillary Action: The spontaneous rising of a liquid up a narrow tube.

Capillary action can be observed when pacing a narrow tube into a liquid with strong intermolecular forces. It is a result of two processes: adhesive forces between the liquid and container pulls the liquid up the walls of the tube, wetting them; cohesive forces within the liquid draw the liquid up the tube to decrease the surface area. In this way, surface tension plays a large role in the ability of a liquid to experience capillary action.

Viscosity: A measure of a fluid's resistance to deformation at a given rate.

Some liquids are noticeably "thicker" than others. Strong intermolecular forces in a liquid cause the liquid to resist changing shape quickly when poured.

1.10 In the following substances, list the *dominant* intermolecular force.

a) water (H_2O)

b) dimethyl ether (CH_3OCH_3)

c) hexane (C_6H_{14})

d) acetone

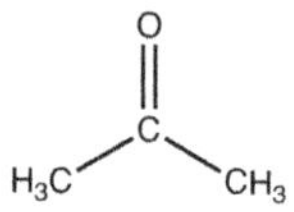

e) ethanol (C_2H_5OH)

f) liquid CO_2

Part 2: Phase Changes

Vaporization and Vapor Pressure

Intermolecular forces influence properties such as boiling point, vapor pressure, viscosity, and surface tension. Boiling point and vapor pressure are closely linked to changes of state: solid → liquid → gas. Energy must be added to a substance to melt or vaporize it...how much energy you need is determined by the intermolecular forces.

2.1 When water is boiling on a stove, heat is being added, but the temperature remains constant. Why doesn't the temperature continue to rise as heat is continuously added?

The energy we add to a substance in order to change its state can be measured. Let's define a few of these terms:

Heat of fusion (ΔH_{fus}): The energy needed to melt 1 mol of a solid.

Heat of vaporization (ΔH_{vap}): The energy needed to vaporize 1 mol of a liquid to gas.

Some substances do not need to pass from solid to liquid to gas (dry ice, CO_2 (s) is an example). The process of going from solid directly to gas is called *sublimation* (the opposite direction, gas-to-solid is called *deposition*).

So now we have some terms we can use to describe the phase changes that are possible when moving between solid, liquid, and gas.

2.2 Fill in the following chart with the corresponding terms for the phase changes shown.

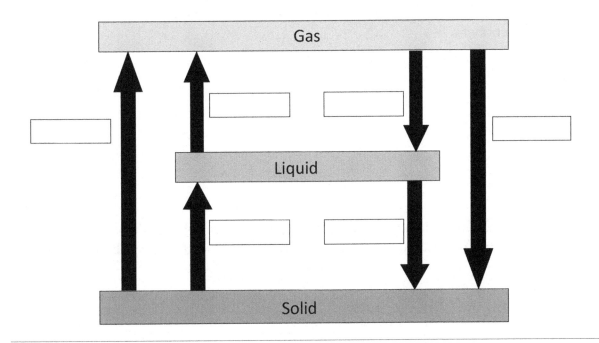

Vapor Pressure

Let's start to understand phase changes by looking at boiling (or evaporation/vaporization): the change from liquid to gas. Molecules in the liquid phase must gain enough kinetic energy to overcome the intermolecular forces and escape into the gas phase. We can use vapor pressure as a measure of a liquid's intermolecular forces.

When a sealed flask containing a liquid is allowed to sit, it eventually reaches equilibrium. At this point the rate of vaporization of the liquid is equal to the rate of condensation. That means for every molecule that escapes into the gas phase, one returns to the liquid phase. The pressure of the vapor at equilibrium is called the vapor pressure (P_{vap}) and can be thought of as the pressure of the gas molecules pushing down on the liquid. When the vapor pressure of a substance is high (a lot of molecules in the gas phase), we call that substance *volatile*.

2.3 Remembering what you learned about intermolecular forces, list the following compounds in order from lowest vapor pressure (least volatile) to highest vapor pressure (most volatile). *Note: All three compounds have molar masses that range from 46-58 g/mol.*

methyl chloride (CH_3Cl), ethanol (C_2H_5OH), butane (C_4H_{10})

The vapor pressure of a substance is influenced by temperature, since vapor pressure is related to the kinetic energy of the molecules. As we raise the temperature, more molecules enter the gas phase and the vapor pressure rises. Eventually, if we continue to raise the temperature, the vapor pressure of the substance will reach the vapor pressure of the external pressure. At this point, the substance boils. Put another way, we can find the **boiling point** of any substance: it is the temperature at which the vapor pressure of the substance is equal to the external pressure.

2.4 The atmospheric pressure at sea level is about 1 atm. In Denver, Colorado, the atmospheric pressure is about 0.8 atm. Would you expect the boiling point of water to be the same or different in these two places? Explain your answer briefly.

Since boiling point and pressure are related, it's helpful to report the **normal boiling point** of liquids: the temperature at which a substance's vapor pressure equals 1 atm. For water, the normal boiling point is 100 °C.

Enthalpy of Phase Changes

As we saw before, ΔH_{vap} is the energy needed to vaporize 1 mol of a liquid to gas. We can utilize our definition of "standard" (1 atm of pressure) to define the standard heat of vaporization ($\Delta H°_{vap}$) as the energy needed to vaporize 1 mol of a liquid to gas at 1 atm of pressure.

For water, $\Delta H°_{vap}$ = +40.7 kJ/mol. It requires 40.7 kJ of heat to vaporize one mole of water at 1 atm of pressure at 100 °C. At lower temperatures more energy is required (since the water contains less thermal energy).

It turns out we can use the relationship between vapor pressure and temperature to find the heat of vaporization for any substance. The **Clausius-Clapeyron Equation** relates pressure and temperature in the following way:

$$lnP = \frac{-\Delta H_{vap}}{R}\left(\frac{1}{T}\right) + C$$

2.5 This equation is in the form of y = mx + b. If we had measured the vapor pressure of a substance at various temperatures, what plot of the data would give us a straight line? What would the slope be equal to in this case?

2.6 What value / units of R should be used in this equation?

We can further rearrange the Clausius-Clapeyron Equation using just two measurements of P and T:

$$ln\frac{P_1}{P_2} = \frac{\Delta H_{vap}}{R}\left(\frac{1}{T_2} - \frac{1}{T_1}\right)$$

From this equation, the knowledge of any two pressures at two temperatures allows us to calculate ΔH_{vap} for a substance.

2.7 Calculate the heat of vaporization of diethyl ether from the following vapor pressures: 400. mmHg at 18.0 °C and 760. mmHg at 35.0 °C.

2.8 How does the vapor pressure of a substance change with increasing temperature?

Phase Changes and Enthalpy

Every phase change is accompanied by its own enthalpy – the energy required (or released) during the change. Melting and freezing is described by the **heat of fusion** (ΔH_{fus}):

$$H_2O \ (s) \rightarrow H_2O \ (l) \qquad \Delta H_{fus} = + \ 6.02 \ kJ/mol \ \text{(a positive value because melting requires energy)}$$

The opposite process (freezing) *releases* the same amount of energy:

$$H_2O \ (l) \rightarrow H_2O \ (s) \qquad \Delta H_{fus} = - \ 6.02 \ kJ/mol \ \text{(a negative value because freezing releases energy)}$$

We also know that the energy required (or released) when moving between liquid and gas phases is the heat of vaporization. Since enthalpy is a state function, we can determine the amount of heat required to move directly from solid to the gas phase (sublimation):

$$H_2O \ (s) \rightarrow H_2O \ (g) \qquad \Delta H_{sub} = \Delta H_{fus} + \Delta H_{vap} = 6.02 \ kJ/mol + 40.7 \ kJ/mol = 46.7 \ kJ/mol$$

2.9 Benzene (C_6H_6) has the following thermodynamic data: $\Delta H_{fus} = 9.9 \ kJ/mol$, $\Delta H_{vap} = 30.7 \ kJ/mol$. How much energy is required to sublime one mole of benzene from solid to gas?

Phase Diagrams

2.10 Label the following generic phase diagram with the proper terms:

Phase Diagram (Generic)

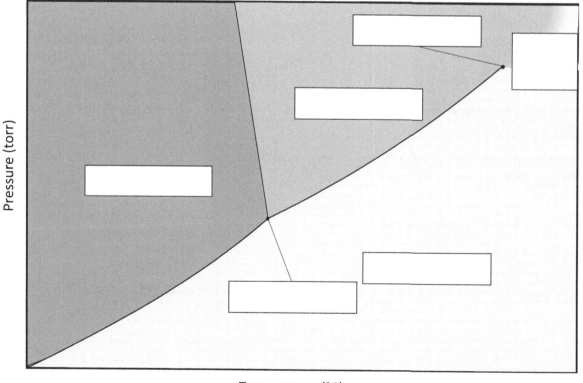

2.11 Define the following terms:

a) Triple point:

b) Critical point:

c) Supercritical fluid:

2.12 Using the diagram above, what sequence of phases do you encounter if you move from low pressure to higher pressure at low temperature? What if you repeat the process at a moderately higher temperature?

Part 3: Solutions and Solubility

Solutions are mixtures of substances and can occur in a variety of phases. We typically think of solutions as having two components: the **solute** and the **solvent**.

3.1 List at least four solutions from your daily life. What would you consider the solvent and what would you consider the solute in each of these solutions?

Solution	Solvent	Solute

3.2 Can you think of some examples of two things that you could try to mix, but would not create a uniform solution?

In order for a solution to form between two or more substances, primarily in the liquid phase, the solvent-solute interactions must be comparable or stronger than the interactions between the solvent or the solute particles alone. This means that the intermolecular forces must be similar for two substances to mix. For example, non-polar substances tend to experience only dispersion forces. Since dispersion forces are of similar strength among non-polar substances, these tend to mix together fairly evenly. On the other hand, in order to mix a non-polar substance like vegetable oil (mostly dispersion forces) with a polar substance like water (hydrogen-bonding forces), you have to break up the strong hydrogen bonds between the water molecules to let the oil particles in. Since the resulting interactions are weaker than the original ones, this process is not very favorable and the oil and water separate back out again.

3.3 We usually summarize this tendency for similar substances to mix with the phrase "*like dissolves like*". Summarize what this phrase means (in your own words) with respect to polar and non-polar substances.

3.4 Predict which solvent will dissolve more of the given solute.

   a) Sodium chloride: Will more dissolve in methanol (CH_3OH) or in propanol ($CH_3CH_2CH_2OH$)?

   b) Ethylene glycol ($HOCH_2CH_2OH$): Will more dissolve in water or in hexane (C_6H_{14})?

   c) Diethyl ether ($CH_3CH_2OCH_2CH_3$): will more dissolve in ethanol (CH_3CH_2OH) or in water?

Energetics of Solution Formation

Sometimes mixing a solution results in a change in temperature. In some cases the solution gets hot, other times it gets cold. Sometimes there is no change in temperature at all. How can we explain these observations - or better yet, predict them? To do that, we need to understand the solution cycle.

The solution cycle can be described in three steps, each with its own thermodynamic properties:

   Step 1: The solute is separated into components. This step **requires** energy to overcome the intermolecular forces of the solute and expand it to make room for the solvent. As a result, this step is endothermic:

   ($\Delta H_{solute} > 0$).

   Step 2: The solvent is separated into components. This step **requires** energy to overcome the intermolecular forces of the solvent and expand it to make room for the solute. As a result, this step is endothermic:

   ($\Delta H_{solvent} > 0$).

   Step 3: the solvent and solute particles mix. The individual particles attract each other and **give off energy** as they interact. This step is exothermic:

   ($\Delta H_{mix} < 0$)

If the magnitude of the enthalpy of the endothermic steps is less than that of the exothermic step (mixing) then the solution becomes warmer. The excess heat is given off by the system to the surroundings.

If the magnitude of the enthalpy of the endothermic steps is more than that of the exothermic step (mixing) then the solution becomes colder. Heat is absorbed by the system from the surroundings.

3.5 Sketch two energy diagrams: one for an exothermic solution cycle and one for an endothermic solution cycle.

Gas Solubility

In solutions made of gases dissolved in water, the solubility of the gas depends on two major factors: temperature and pressure. Most sample of water that you have experience with have gases dissolved in them – even just leaving a glass of water out in the open will result in nitrogen and oxygen being dissolved into it. Other solutions with gases dissolved in them include soda (carbon dioxide), lake and ocean water (oxygen and nitrogen), and your blood (oxygen, nitrogen, and carbon dioxide).

Effect of Temperature on the Solubility of Gases

Since gases, for the most part, do not tend to interact with the solvent in gas/liquid solutions, **increases in temperature result in lower gas solubility.** Increasing the temperature of the solution results in higher kinetic energy of the gas particles, causing them to leave the solution at much higher rates than at colder temperatures.

Effect of Pressure on the Solubility of Gases

The amount of gas dissolved in a solution is directly proportional to the pressure of the gas above the solution. The higher the pressure of the gas above the solution, the more gas particles will be forced into the solution and dissolved. As the pressure of the gas is decreased, the gas particles escape again and the solubility decreases. This relationship can be summarized by Henry's Law:

$$S_{gas} = k_H P_{gas}$$

Here S_{gas} represents the solubility of the gas (in M, mol/L), P_{gas} is the partial pressure of the gas above the solution, and k_H is the constant characteristic of the solution (Henry's Law Constant).

3.6 What is the solubility of oxygen gas in water at 25 °C at 1.0 atm pressure of air (which is 20.9% oxygen)? The Henry's Law constant for O_2 in water is 1.3×10^{-3} M/atm.

3.7 Would you expect this solubility to go up or down if the temperature is increased from 25 °C to 50 °C?

Concentration Revisited – Other Units of Concentration

We have previously used molarity (M, mol of solute in L of solution) as a measure of solution concentration. There are actually many different ways to measure concentration. Here are a few more:

Molarity: $\dfrac{mol\ of\ solute}{volume\ (L)\ of\ solvent}$

Molality (m): $\dfrac{mol\ of\ solute}{mass\ (kg)\ of\ solvent}$

Parts by mass: $\dfrac{mass\ of\ solute}{mass\ of\ solution}$

Parts by volume: $\dfrac{volume\ of\ solute}{mvolume\ of\ solution}$

mole fraction (X): $\dfrac{mol\ of\ solute}{mol\ of\ solute\ +\ mol\ solvent}$

3.8 Give the concentration of 29.3 g of Na_2SO_4 in 275 mL of water (density = 1 g/mL) in the following ways:

a) molarity

b) molality

c) parts sodium sulfate by mass

d) mole fraction of Na_2SO_4 in water

Part 4: Colligative Properties

When we dissolve non-volatile solutes (solids like sugar or salt) into solvents, it changes many of the properties of the solvent. The properties that change are collectively called colligative properties. These properties depend only on the number of molecules dissolved in the solvent and not on the properties of the solute itself. When we dissolve a substance into a solvent we observe the following changes:

Vapor pressure of the solvent is lowered

Boiling point of the solvent is raised

Freezing point of the solvent is lowered

Osmotic pressure is developed

Let's look at each of these changes in terms of why they happen and to what extent they change the properties of our solvent.

Vapor Pressure Lowering

When a *non-volatile, non-electrolyte* solute (like sugar) is added to a solvent (like water) the vapor pressure of the solvent is lowered.

4.1 Describe the vapor pressure of a liquid like water in terms of molecules moving from the liquid phase to the solid phase. What does this look like at the surface of the liquid (liquid/gas interface)?

4.2 The presence of solute particles at the surface of the liquid decreases the number of solvent particles at the surface. How would this affect the rate of evaporation of solvent?

The new, reduced vapor pressure of the solvent (in the solution) can be calculated according to Raoult's Law:

$$P_{solution} = X_{solvent}P^{\circ}_{solvent}$$

In this equation, $X_{solvent}$ is the mole fraction of the solvent.

4.3 Recall what the mole fraction of a substance is and write an expression for the mole fraction of solvent in a solution.

4.4 What is the mole fraction of water in a solution that has 1.0 mole of sugar (342.3 g/mol) dissolved in 0.45 L of water (450 g; about 25 moles)?

4.5 If the vapor pressure of pure water at 25 °C is 23.8 mmHg, what is the vapor pressure of the solution in the previous question at the same temperature?

We can rearrange Raoult's Law to find the change (lowering) in vapor pressure (ΔP) in terms of the mole fraction of the solute (X_{solute}):

$$\Delta P = X_{solute} P^{\circ}_{solvent}$$

Either equation can help you determine the change in vapor pressure of your solvent, since $\Delta P = P^{\circ}_{solvent} - P_{solution}$

4.6 What is the mole fraction of **sugar** in the sugar water solution above that has 1.0 mole of sugar dissolved in 25 moles of water?

4.7 What is the vapor-pressure lowering (ΔP) for the solution above? (Pure water still has a vapor pressure of 23.8 mmHg.)

4.8 What is the resulting vapor pressure of the solution, based on your answer to the previous question? Did you get the same answer as when you used the other equation?

What if the solute in your solution is a volatile substance on its own, with its own vapor pressure? How would that affect the solution and what is the result? This is actually a very common occurrence. Anytime we mix two liquids we can experience this. For example, alcohol and water, vinegar and water, and solvent mixtures such as acetone and methanol all are solutions with two volatile components. In cases where the solute and solvent are similar in terms of intermolecular forces, we can expect good agreement with Raoult's Law (these are called ideal solutions). In a solution made of two liquids, A and B, Raoult's Law tells us that:

$$P_A = X_A P^°_A$$

$$\text{and } P_B = X_B P^°_B$$

Additionally, Dalton's Law of Partial Pressure tells us that:

$$P_{total} = P_A + P_B$$

What this means is that the vapor above the solution is just a weighted average of the individual parts of the solution. At higher mole fractions of A, the vapor is enriched with A and *vice versa*. Also, if one substance is much more volatile than the other, we'll see higher amounts of that vapor at similar mole fractions.

4.9 Water is not very volatile ($P^° = 23.8$ mmHg at 25 °C), but the vapor pressure of ethanol at the same temperature is 60.8 mmHg.

   a) What is the vapor pressure of each substance if we have a 50/50 mix of the two liquids by moles (for example, 18 g of water and 46 g of ethanol)?

   b) What is the total pressure of the vapor above this solution? (Hint: $P_{total} = P_{H2O} + P_{ethanol}$)

c) What is the mole fraction of the ethanol in this vapor mix? Is it greater, less, or equal to the 50% we started with in the solution?

d) Why does the vapor above the solution have more ethanol in it than the solution does?

Boiling Point Elevation and Freezing Point Depression

Since boiling point is closely tied to vapor pressure, we can extend our understanding of vapor-pressure lowering to its impact on the boiling point of a solution. Remember that the boiling point of a solution is reached when the vapor pressure of the pure substance is equal to the atmospheric pressure, allowing molecules to escape the gas phase and become gaseous.

4.10 If the vapor pressure of a solution is *lower* than the pure solvent, is more or less heat required to reach a vapor pressure equal to the atmospheric pressure in a solution (compared to the pure substance)?

We can calculate the change in boiling point for a solution (compared to the pure substance) using the following formula:

$$\Delta T_b = mK_b$$

where m is the molality of the solution and K_b is the molal boiling point constant for the solvent.

Similarly, the presence of solute lowers the rate at which molecules in the liquid phase return to solid at the freezing point. As a result, the freezing point of a solution is lowered compared to the pure solvent. The change in freezing point can be found by:

$$\Delta T_f = mK_f$$

where m is again molality and K_f is the molal freezing point constant for the solvent.

Overall, the presence of a solute extends the liquid range of the solution – raising the boiling point and lowering the freezing point.

A table of common solvents and their molal freezing and boiling point constants is given here:

Solvent	Normal Freezing Point (°C)	K_f (°C/m)	Normal Boiling Point (°C)	K_b (°C/m)
water	0.00	1.86	100.0	0.512
ethanol	-114.1	1.99	78.3	1.22
benzene	5.5	5.12	80.1	2.53
chloroform	-63.5	4.70	61.2	3.63

4.11 Hospitals use saline solutions (0.159 m NaCl in water) to deliver medications intravenously. What is the freezing point and boiling point of this solution?

Osmotic Pressure

The final colligative property we'll examine is a little bit different, but no less important to chemical and biological processes. When we have two solutions with different concentrations of solute in contact with each other, osmosis is the flow of solvent from the solution of lower concentration to one of higher concentration. In general, this flow leads to more uniform concentration throughout. Osmosis is especially important in cellular processes. Placing a cell into a solution with much higher (or much lower) concentrations of solutes will result in the flow of solvent (water) either out of or into the cell. The cell wall acts as a semi-permeable membrane – a substance that allows only some substances to pass through. Let's explore a more controlled, simpler experimental set-up.

Here we have two solutions separated by a semi-permeable membrane. One solution has solute particles in it, while the other half of the tube contains pure water. The membrane allows water to flow, but does not allow the solute particles to pass through. The water molecules spontaneously flow through the membrane to the area of higher solute concentration. As this happens the water levels change. The water level on the solution side climbs while the water level on the pure water side drops. The difference in height of these two sides leads to what we call osmotic pressure – the pressure required to stop the osmotic flow.

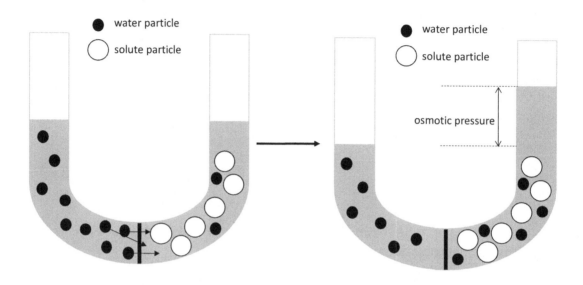

The osmotic pressure (Π) depends on the molarity (M) of the solution and the temperature (T) and can be calculated by:

$$\Pi = MRT$$

Osmotic pressure is often used to find the molar mass of unknown solutes, but is also responsible for the swelling of red blood cells when placed in pure water.

4.12 The concentration of solutes in a red blood cell is about a third that of seawater – about 0.3 M. If red blood cells are immersed in pure water, they swell. Calculate the osmotic pressure at 25 °C of red blood cells across the cell membrane from pure water.

Strong Electrolyte Solutions

As we have seen, the number of solute particles in a solution influences the properties. When we dissolve strong electrolytes in a solution we have to remember that our ionic compounds dissociate into more particles than non-electrolyte solutes (for example, a molecule of NaCl creates two particles in solution, Na^+ and Cl^-, while a molecule of sugar creates only a single particle). In order to account for this, we can update our formulas for instances when we have strong electrolytes in solution. In order to do so, we have to introduce the van't Hoff factor (i):

$$i = \frac{moles\ of\ particles\ in\ solution}{moles\ of\ formula\ units\ dissolved}$$

4.13 Give the van't Hoff factor for the following strong electrolytes (assume full dissociation):

a) NaCl : _____   b) $MgCl_2$: _____   c) LiF : _____

d) $MgSO_4$: _____   e) $FeCl_3$: _____   f) sugar : _____

We can use revised formulas for freezing point depression, boiling point elevation, and osmotic pressure:

$$\text{Freezing point depression: } \Delta T_f = imK_f$$

$$\text{Boiling point elevation: } \Delta T_b = imK_b$$

$$\text{Osmotic Pressure: } \Pi = iMRT$$

For vapor pressure our adjustments are not quite as simple, since we work in mole fraction. We include the van't Hoff factor in the mole fraction calculation in the following way:

$$X_{solvent} = \frac{n_{solvent}}{i \times n_{solute} + n_{solvent}}$$

4.14 If 1.00 mole of $MgCl_2$ (95.2 g) is dissolved in 25 moles of water (0.45 L, 450 g), what is the freezing point, boiling point, osmotic pressure, and vapor pressure of the solution (all at 25 °C)?

Concept Map

Create a concept map using the following key words. You may add any additional words, as necessary.

solute	solvent	solids	liquids	gases
dispersion forces	dipole-dipole forces	hydrogen bonds	polar substances	non-polar substances
boiling point	freezing point	vaporization	melting	condensation
sublimation	deposition	freezing	enthalpy	solubility
vapor pressure lowering	freezing point depression	boiling point elevation	osmotic pressure	electrolytes

Unit 8

Molecular Orbital Theory

Part 1: Introduction to Molecular Orbitals

Limitations of Valence Bond Theory

Warm-Up Exercises

1.1. Draw a Lewis dot structure of oxygen (O_2). Does your structure show all electrons paired?

1.2. Draw Lewis dot structures of the following molecules (all are actual compounds that have been made in a lab):

   a) H_2^+

   b) NO

   c) He_2^+

   Is it difficult to create these structures using our typical rules for Lewis dot structures?

1.3. Draw Lewis dot structures for CO and N_2. Does your structure explain why the bond dissociation energy (BDE: energy required to break the bonds) for CO is 1,076 kJ/mol while the BDE for N_2 is 945 kJ/mol?

Molecular Orbitals and Molecular Orbital Diagrams

While Lewis dot structures and molecular hybridization are excellent, simple models used to describe bonding, you can see that there are circumstances when these models fail to help us explain certain observations. For example, valence bond theory (the term we use to refer to Lewis dot structures and hybridization) does not adequately explain magnetic properties of molecules, odd-electron species, and the bond energy of molecules. When one model fails us, it's time to turn to a better model. That model now is **molecular orbital theory**.

Molecular orbital (MO) theory is based on many of the same principles we have already learned. The basic premise is that atomic orbitals (1s, 2s, 2p, etc.) interact to form a bond and the result is the formation of new orbitals: molecular orbitals.

The fundamental principle relies on the constructive and destructive interference of waves – specifically, the constructive and destructive interference of atomic orbital standing wavefunctions.

Recall these questions from our unit of quantum mechanics:

1.4 Show the resulting wave if the following two waves are added together. Is this constructive or destructive interference?

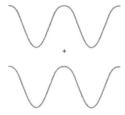

1.5 Show the resulting wave if the following two waves are added together. Is this constructive or destructive interference?

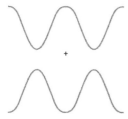

When the waves of two s orbitals interact (such as what happens when two hydrogen atoms approach each other), they can interfere constructively or destructively:

Constructive interference of two s orbitals:

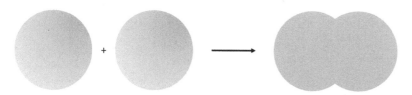

Destructive interference of two s orbitals:

These new *molecular* orbitals behave in the same manner we treat atomic orbitals: we fill them in order of lowest to highest energy (Aufbau principle), they each hold two electron (Pauli exclusion principle), and we spread electrons out among degenerate orbitals before pairing electrons (Hund's rule). Likewise, the square of the wavefunction gives us the likely region in space we might find an electron.

A slight difference is that we must conserve the number of orbitals we have and their total energy. This means that if we combine two atomic orbitals, we get two molecular orbitals, one lower in energy and one higher in energy than our original atomic orbitals. We can illustrate this process with a molecular orbital diagram:

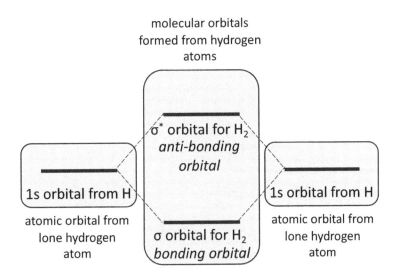

Each hydrogen atom brings one electron, so we put two total electrons into our molecular orbital diagram, filling from the bottom (lowest energy) up. For H_2, this means there are two electrons (with opposite spins) in the σ (bonding) orbital. The higher energy σ^* (anti-bonding) orbital is empty. The electrons are paired and the molecular orbital has an overall lower energy than the separate atomic orbitals, reflecting the lower overall potential energy that H_2 has compared to separate hydrogen atoms.

We can define the **bond order** of a molecule using this molecular orbital diagram as an example:

$$bond\ order = \frac{\#\ of\ electrons\ in\ bonding\ orbitals - \#\ of\ electrons\ in\ antibonding\ orbitals}{2}$$

1.6 What is the bond order for H_2? Does this agree with our result from the Lewis dot structure for H_2?

The power that molecular orbital theory gives us is the ability to understand odd-electron species and less-stable, less-typical molecules. For example, let's explore the molecules He_2, He_2^+, and H_2^+.

1.7 Fill in the molecular orbital diagrams for each of the molecule shown. Give the bond order for each molecule and predict if they might have a possible existence.

a) He_2

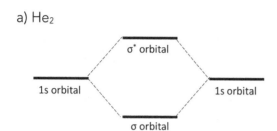

Bond order: _____

b) He_2^+

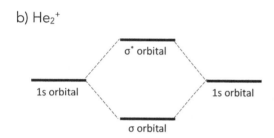

Bond order: _____

c) H_2^+

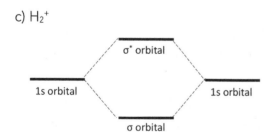

Bond order: _____

As you can see, fractional bond orders are possible. These reflect weaker bonds than full bond orders. For example, while H_2 has a bond dissociation energy of 436 kJ/mol, H_2^+ has a much lower bond energy of 255 kJ/mol.

Another benefit of MO Theory is its ability to predict magnetic properties. Let's define two terms:

Diamagnetic. A diamagnetic molecule contains only **paired** electrons and **is not attracted** to an applied magnetic field.

Paramagnetic. A paramagnetic molecule contains **unpaired** electrons and **is attracted** to an applied magnetic field.

1.8 Which of the molecules, in the question above, would be paramagnetic?

Part 2: Molecular Orbital Theory with p Orbitals

We have looked at the simple case of how **σ-bonds** are formed through the interaction of s orbitals. We also have to consider how bonds can form using p orbitals. This introduces another type of bonding mode to consider: π bonds. Both types of bonds (**σ** and **π**) can be formed by p orbitals interacting with each other. Let's define the difference before illustrating how they can be formed.

> **σ-bonds** are formed by the overlap / interaction of two orbitals in a way that puts electrons density in the space directly between the two nuclei (the **inter-nuclear axis**). This can occur through the interaction of two s orbitals, an s orbital and a p orbital, or two p orbitals.

> **π-bonds** are formed by the overlap / interaction of two orbitals that puts electron density **above and below the inter-nuclear axis** (but not directly between the two nuclei). This occurs through the interaction of two p orbitals.

Below are some examples of how p orbitals can interact to form **σ** and **π** bonds:

σ-bonds formed by two $2p_x$ orbitals:

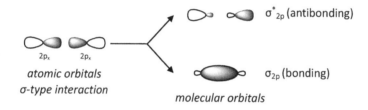

π-bonds formed by two $2p_z$ orbitals and two $2p_y$ orbitals:

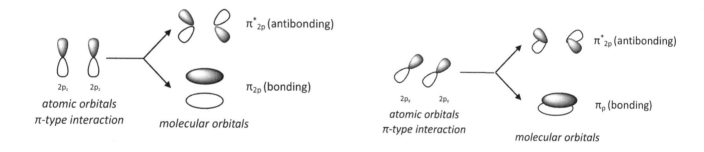

2.1 in the illustrations above, add dots to indicate the nuclei of the two atoms joined by the bond in both the atomic orbitals and the molecular orbitals. Draw a line to show the "inter-nuclear axis" in each set of molecular orbitals.

Let's see how s and p orbitals can interact in a molecule like N_2 using a more complex MO diagram. (Note: this is the generic MO diagram for the diatomics B_2, C_2, and N_2.

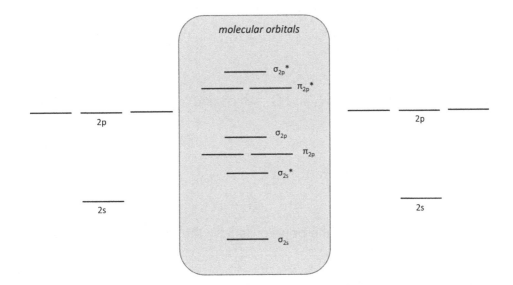

To fill this orbital diagram, we simply add enough electrons (using the same rules we always have for orbital filling) with the correct number of electrons.

2.2 How many valence electrons should be used in the Lewis dot structure for N_2? This is the same number of electrons we will use to fill our MO diagram, above. Fill the MO diagram with the correct number of electrons. What is the calculated bond order for N_2? Is this consistent with the Lewis dot structure for N_2?

Moving forward, we will just use the central portion of the MO diagram, for simplicity (shown in the gray box for N_2 in the previous example).

The generic MO diagram for O_2 and F_2 is a little different, due to the difference in energy levels of the 2s and 2p orbitals in the atoms:

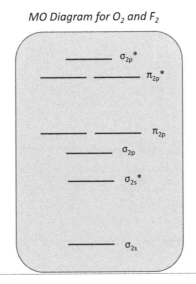

MO Diagram for O_2 and F_2

2.3 How many valence electrons should be used in the Lewis dot structure for O_2? This is the same number of electrons we will use to fill our MO diagram, above. Fill the MO diagram with the correct number of electrons. What is the calculated bond order for O_2? Is this consistent with the Lewis dot structure for O_2?

2.4 Looking at your filled orbital diagrams for N_2 and O_2, which one molecule(s) would you predict to be paramagnetic?

2.5 Using the proper MO diagrams, calculate the bond orders for the following molecules:

a) N_2^+ bond order: _____

b) O_2^+ bond order: _____

c) Which of the ions, above, would you expect to be *more* stable than their neutral relatives? Why? What type of orbital is the missing electron in each ion coming from?

Part 3: Heteronuclear Molecular Orbitals

Warm-Up Exercises

3.1. Write a brief definition of electronegativity.

3.2. Would you expect an electron in an orbital near an electronegative atom to be relatively higher or lower in potential energy (less or more stable) than near a less electronegative atom? Why?

3.3. Sketch a rough diagram of the periodic table with an arrow depicting the general trend in electronegativity.

Heteronuclear Diatomic Molecular Orbital Diagrams

When atoms differ in electronegativity we need to adjust our molecular orbital diagram to reflect the different "pull" each atom has on the electrons in the bond. To do this, we draw the more electronegative atom orbital lower in energy than the less electronegative atom. Here's an example with HF:

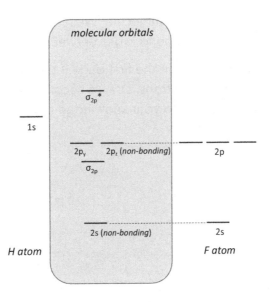

You will notice that not all the orbitals are involved in bonding – some fluorine orbitals do not interact with the hydrogen 1s orbital. This is because the orbitals are either a) too different in energy or b) do not overlap in space enough to interact.

3.4 Fill in the MO diagram with the correct number of valence electron for HF.

a) What is the bond order for this molecule?

b) How many non-bonding **pairs** of electrons are present in the molecule? How does this relate to the number of lone pairs in the Lewis dot structure of HF?

c) When a molecular orbital is closer in energy to an orbital on the "parent" atom we say the electrons in the orbital reside in an orbital "like" that atom. Do the electrons in the H-F bond reside in a more hydrogen-like or fluorine-like orbital? Does this answer agree with your understanding of electronegativity?

Let's revisit the problem of NO, an odd-electron molecule. While Lewis dot structures suggest a bond order of two, experimental evidence suggest a bond order between two and three.

3.5 Look back at your answer to question 1.2b on the first page if this unit. Redraw here your Lewis dot structure for NO, a species with 11 valence electrons. Draw a second Lewis dot structure where the lone electron resides on the other atom. According to your knowledge of Lewis dot structures, which is most likely correct?

3.6 Fill in the MO diagram for NO, shown below, with the correct number of electrons. What is the bond order for NO? What type of orbital does the lone electron reside in – N-like or O-like? Does this agree with your "best" Lewis dot structure? Does your MO diagram agree with the experimental evidence for the bond order?

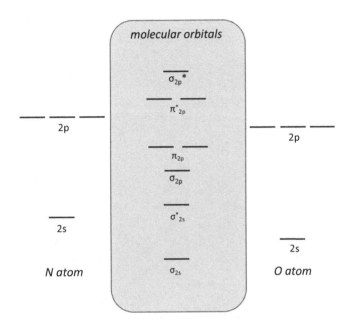

Made in the USA
Las Vegas, NV
23 August 2021